I0009801

TABLE OF CONTENTS

APPENDICES

U.S. COPYRIGHT OFFICE

REPORT ON LEGAL PROTECTION FOR DATABASES

August 1997

Introduction

Databases have always been commodities of both commercial value and social utility, ranging from their early incarnation in the eighteenth century as directories compiled by walking door to door to the late twentieth-century compendiums of millions of items in electronic form. The question of whether and how databases should be protected by the law has never been easy, as it necessarily involves finding a balance between two potentially conflicting societal goals: the goal of providing adequate incentives for their continued production, and the goal of ensuring public access to the information they contain. At different points in time, and in different societies, that balance has been struck in different ways.

In the past few years, the issue has taken on new urgency due to changes in the legal, technological and international landscape. The major landmarks among these changes have been the U.S. Supreme Court's 1991 decision in *Feist Publications v. Rural Telephone Service Co.*; rapid developments in the technologies for collecting, organizing, reproducing and disseminating information; and the actions of the European Union in harmonizing the laws of its member states. As a result, 1996 saw the consideration of proposals for a new form of protection for databases, both in the World Intellectual Property Organization and in the U.S. Congress. The discussions sparked a heated debate in the United States, involving a broad spectrum of interests.

In early 1997, the Copyright Office initiated its own examination of database protection by scheduling meetings with several groups that had expressed opposition to the 1996 proposals, in

1

order to gain a clearer understanding of their concerns. In April, Senator Orrin G. Hatch, Chairman of the Senate Committee on the Judiciary, requested that the Office broaden its meetings to include a wide range of interested parties, and report to the Judiciary Committee on the outcome in order to assist in the Committee's consideration of the subject. Since that time, the House Subcommittee on Courts and Intellectual Property, chaired by Rep. Howard Coble, has also asked to see the report in connection with its own consideration.

The purpose of this report is to provide some background and context to the subject of database protection, to identify and clarify the issues involved, and generally to lay the initial groundwork for a Congressional determination of appropriate legislative policy. The report is divided into seven substantive sections: (1) an historical overview of copyright protection for databases in the United States; (2) a description of database industry practices in securing protection against unauthorized use; (3) a description of Copyright Office registration practices relating to databases; (4) a summary of the relevant international context, focusing on the European database directive and the draft WIPO treaty on the protection of databases; (5) a summary of prior Congressional consideration of the subject; (6) a description of the methodology and substance of the meetings held by the Copyright Office; and (7) a discussion of the issues presented.

The report does not make recommendations on either the advisability or the form of any database protection legislation. At this point, we seek only to present the issues to be addressed, and to offer some options for addressing specific concerns. Their resolution will await public hearings and the presentation of evidence.

I. COPYRIGHT PROTECTION FOR DATABASES IN THE UNITED STATES

A.   Before *Feist*

In the terminology of copyright law, a database is a "compilation": "a work formed by the

collection and assembling of preexisting materials or of data . . . ."[1] Compilations constitute one

of the oldest forms of authorship protected under U.S. law, dating back to the eighteenth

century.[2] Compilations were protected as "books" under the first federal copyright statute.[3]

Over the course of the nineteenth century two rationales developed for protecting

compilations under copyright. One rationale, which has come to be known as the "sweat of the

brow" doctrine, focused on the effort and investment of the compiler. The other focused on the

compiler's judgment and creativity in the selection and arrangement of the materials comprising

the compilation.

The earliest compilation cases that discussed the basis for copyright protection identified

the compiler's effort — "his own expense, or skill, or labor, or money"[4] — as the critical

contribution justifying protection.[5] These cases, involving works ranging from law reports and

---

[1] 17 U.S.C. § 101.

[2] *See, e.g.,* Kilty v. Green, 4 H. & McH. 345 (Gen. Ct. Md. 1799) (denying relief in case involving compilation of statutes).

[3] Copyright Act of May 31, 1790, ch. 15, 1 Stat. 124 (protecting books, maps and charts).

[4] Emerson v. Davies, 8 F. Cas. 615, 619 (C.C.D. Mass. 1845).

[5] *See, e.g.,* Dun v. Lumbermen's Credit Assoc., 144 F. 83 (7th Cir. 1906), *aff'd*, 209 U.S. 20 (1908); West Pub. Co. v. Lawyers' Co-operative Pub. Co., 79 F. 756 (2d Cir. 1897); West Pub. Co. v. Edward Thompson Co., 169 F. 833 (C.C.E.D.N.Y. 1909), *modified*, 176 F. 833 (2d Cir. 1910); Egbert v. Greenberg, 100 F. 447 (C.C.N.D. Cal. 1900); Ladd v. Oxnard, 75 F. 703 (C.C.D. Mass. 1896); American Trotting Register Assoc. v. Gocher, 70 F. 237 (C.C.N.D. Ohio 1895); Hanson v. Jaccard Jewelry Co., 32 F. 202 (C.C.E.D. Mo. 1887); Chapman v. Ferry, 18 F. 539 (C.C.D. Oreg. 1883); Banks v. McDivitt, 2 F. Cas. 759, 13 Blatchf. 163 (C.C.S.D.N.Y. 1875); Webb v. Powers, 29 F. Cas. 511 (C.C.D. Mass. 1847); Emerson v. Davies, 8 F. Cas. 615 (C.C.D. Mass. 1845); Gray v. Russell, 10 F. Cas. 1035 (C.C.D. Mass. 1839).

legal encyclopedias to compilations of war records, emphasized both the compilers' effort and the copiers' "unfair use of the copyrighted work, in order to save themselves the time and labor of original investigation."[6] Contemporary treatises echoed this approach.[7]

During the late nineteenth century courts began to articulate a basis for copyright protection generally that differed from the labor/investment approach taken in cases involving compilations. In a series of decisions from 1879 to 1903, the Supreme Court held that the "writings" that could be protected under the copyright clause of the Constitution included "only such as are original,"[8] and indicated that creativity is a component of originality.[9] Under this approach, copyright was described as protecting writings that are "the fruits of intellectual labor,"[10] "productions of intellect or genius"[11] or "original intellectual conceptions of the author."[12]

The evolving doctrine of originality was applied by some courts in compilation cases, particularly cases involving compilations of textual materials such as law books. These cases identified the author's critical contribution justifying protection as his judgment in selecting and

---

[6] *West Pub. Co., 79 F. at 772.*

[7] *See, e.g.,* EATON S. DRONE, A TREATISE ON THE LAW OF PROPERTY IN INTELLECTUAL PRODUCTIONS IN GREAT BRITAIN AND THE UNITED STATES 386 (1879); GEORGE T. CURTIS, TREATISE ON THE LAW OF COPYRIGHT 174 (1847).

[8] *In re* The Trademark Cases, 100 U.S. 82, 94 (1879).

[9] Bleistein v. Donaldson Lithographing Co., 188 U.S. 239 (1903); Higgins v. Keuffel, 140 U.S. 428 (1891); Burrow-Giles Lithographic Co. v. Sarony, 111 U.S. 53 (1884); *In re* The Trademark Cases, 100 U.S. at 94. *See also* National Tel. News Co. v. Western Union Tel. Co., 119 F. 294 (7th Cir. 1902); Boucicault v. Fox, 3 F. Cas. 977, 5 Blatchf. 87 (C.C.S.D.N.Y. 1862); Reed v. Carusi, 20 F. Cas. 431 (C.C.D. Md. 1845).

[10] *In re* The Trademark Cases, 100 U.S. at 94. *See also Higgins*, 140 U.S. at 431.

[11] American Tobacco Co. v. Werckmeister, 207 U.S. 284, 291 (1907).

[12] *Burrow-Giles*, 111 U.S. at 59-60. *See also* WILLIAM W. ELLSWORTH, A COPY-RIGHT MANUAL 10 (1862) (stating "mere mechanical labor will not suffice; intellectual labor or invention is indispensable").

arranging materials.[13] This approach coexisted with, rather than supplanted, sweat of the brow cases. Sweat of the brow was applied to cases involving purely factual compilations, such as catalogs and directories. Sometimes the two approaches appeared to be melded together in a single case, with the court focusing on the "labor" and "skill" contributed by the author.[14] With very few exceptions, one or the other approach was drawn upon by the court to support the conclusion that a particular compilation was protectible, rather than to deny protection.

On the question of the *scope* of protection afforded to compilations, there was somewhat greater uniformity in the case law. In compilation cases, regardless of the theoretical framework adopted to justify copyright protection, once the plaintiff's work was determined to be copyrightable, courts generally held a defendant to have infringed whenever material was copied from the plaintiff's work. Typically there was no inquiry as to whether the particular material copied was protected by the plaintiff's copyright. To avoid infringement, a second-comer was required to go to the original sources and compile the material independently, without reference to the earlier work.[15] A common thread running through many of these decisions was the court's desire to prevent the copier from competing unfairly with the compiler by appropriating the fruits of the compiler's efforts or creativity. In this sense, courts treated copyright protection for compilations much like a branch of unfair competition law.

The Copyright Act of 1976 included a definition of "compilation" which, for the first time, drew an express statutory connection between compilations and "original works of authorship":

---

[13] *See, e.g.,* Edward Thompson Co. v. American Lawbook Co., 122 F. 922, 924 (2d Cir. 1903) (focusing on "skill and taste of the [plaintiff] in selecting or arranging" materials); Lawrence v. Dana, 15 F. Cas. 26, 28, 4 Cliff. 1 (C.C.D. Mass. 1869) ("copyright may justly be claimed by an author of a book who has taken existing materials from sources common to all writers, and arranged and combined them in a new form, and given them an application unknown before, for the reason that, in so doing, he has exercised skill and discretion in making the selections, arrangement, and combination . . . .").

[14] *See, e.g.,* Hanson v. Jaccard Jewelry Co., 32 F. 202, 203 (C.C.E.D. Mo. 1887).

[15] *See, e.g.,* Williams v. Smythe, 110 F. 961 (C.C.M.D. Pa. 1901); List Publishing Co. v. Keller, 30 F. 772 (C.C.S.D.N.Y. 1887); *Banks,* 2 F. Cas. 759.

A "compilation" is a work formed by the collection and assembling of preexisting materials or of data that are selected, coordinated, or arranged in such a way that the resulting work as a whole constitutes an original work of authorship. The term "compilation" includes collective works.[16]

The definition compels a court to examine the nature of a compilation's "selection, coordination, or arrangement" in order to determine whether the compilation is "an original work of authorship" protectible under section 102(a). In other words, the same originality requirement applies to compilations as to all other works.

A separate section clarified the scope of protection for compilations, specifying that

The copyright in a compilation or derivative work extends only to the material contributed by the author of such work, as distinguished from the preexisting material employed in the work, and does not imply any exclusive right in the preexisting material. The copyright in such work is independent of, and does not affect or enlarge the scope, duration, ownership, or subsistence of, any copyright protection in the preexisting material.[17]

The 1976 Act also codified the idea/expression dichotomy that had been developed by the courts.[18] Section 102(b) provides: "In no case does copyright protection for an original work of authorship extend to any idea, procedure, process, system, method of operation, concept, principle, or discovery, regardless of the form in which it is described, explained, illustrated, or embodied in such work." This language has been interpreted to exclude protection for facts as well.[19]

---

[16] 17 U.S.C. § 101. *See also id.,* definition of "collective work."

[17] 17 U.S.C. § 103(b).

[18] *See* Baker v. Selden, 101 U.S. 99 (1879).

[19] *See* Harper & Row, Publishers, Inc. v. Nation Enters., 471 U.S. 539 (1985); Feist Publications, Inc. v. Rural Tel. Serv. Co., 499 U.S. 340 (1991).

Cases under the 1976 Act were divided about the continuing viability of the sweat of the brow doctrine. Some circuits continued to apply sweat of the brow.[20] Other circuits rejected sweat of the brow, requiring instead that compilations contain sufficient creativity in their "selection, coordination or arrangement" to render them "original works of authorship" entitled to copyright protection.[21] On both sides of this doctrinal divide, however, there was a consistent line of cases upholding the copyrightability of directories.[22] The stage was thus set for Supreme Court consideration of the issue when it granted certiorari in a Tenth Circuit case routinely applying the sweat of the brow doctrine to protect a white pages telephone directory against wholesale copying.[23]

B.   The *Feist* Decision

The Supreme Court sounded the death knell for the sweat of the brow doctrine in *Feist Publications v. Rural Telephone Service Co.*[24] In finding a white pages telephone directory to be uncopyrightable, the Court held that the sole basis for protection under U.S. copyright law is creative originality.

The plaintiff, Rural Telephone Service Co. (Rural), was a local telephone company that produced a white-pages telephone directory covering its service area. Feist Publications (Feist),

---

[20] *See, e.g.,* Illinois Bell Tel. Co. v. Haines & Co., 683 F. Supp. 1204 (N.D. Ill. 1988), *aff'd*, 905 F.2d 1081 (7th Cir. 1990), *vacated and remanded*, 499 U.S. 944 (1991); Rural Tel. Serv. Co. v. Feist Publications, Inc., 916 F.2d 718 (10th Cir. 1990).

[21] *See, e.g.,* Financial Info., Inc. v. Moody's Investors Serv., Inc., 808 F.2d 204 (2d Cir. 1986), *cert. denied*, 484 U.S. 820 (1987); Eckes v. Card Prices Update, 736 F.2d 859 (2d Cir. 1984); Worth v. Selchow & Righter Co., 827 F.2d 569, 572-73 (9th Cir. 1987).

[22] *See, e.g.,* Hutchinson Tel. Co. v. Fronteer Directory Co. of Minnesota, 770 F.2d 128 (8th Cir. 1985); Southern Bell Tel. and Tel. Co. v. Associated Tel. Directory Publishers, 756 F.2d 801 (11th Cir. 1985).

[23] Feist Publications, Inc. v. Rural Tel. Serv. Co., 916 F.2d 718 (10th Cir. 1990), *cert. granted*, 498 U.S. 808 (1990).

[24] 499 U.S. 340 (1991).

the defendant, published a directory covering multiple service areas. After Feist sought, and was refused, a license to the listings in Rural's directory, it copied the listings without authorization. The district court found Feist liable for infringement, and the Tenth Circuit affirmed in an unpublished memorandum decision. The Supreme Court granted certiorari, presumably to resolve the split in the circuits.[25]

The Court reviewed the history of compilation copyright and the development of the sweat of the brow doctrine. It repudiated the doctrine in unequivocal terms:

> Originality, the Court held, has two distinct components: "independent creation plus a modicum of creativity."[26] The Court emphasized that the creativity component is extremely modest. "To be sure, the requisite level of creativity is extremely low; even a slight amount will suffice. The vast majority of works make the grade quite easily, as they possess some creative spark, 'no matter how crude, humble or obvious' it might be."[27]

The Court reviewed the definition of "compilation" in the Copyright Act of 1976 and discerned an intent to overrule the sweat of the brow doctrine by legislation. By defining a compilation as "a work formed by the collection and assembling of preexisting materials or of data that are selected, coordinated, or arranged in such a way that the resulting work as a whole constitutes an original work of authorship,"[28] the Court explained, Congress specifically required originality in order to protect compilations, and described the elements of authorship that are protected in a compilation: the selection, coordination and arrangement of the underlying material.[29]

---

[25] 498 U.S. 808 (1990).

[26] *Id.* at 346.

[27] *Id.* at 345 (citation omitted).

[28] 17 U.S.C. § 101.

[29] *Feist*, 499 U.S. at 356-58.

The Court did not limit its holding to statutory interpretation, however. It held that "[o]riginality is a constitutional requirement."[30] Citing nineteenth-century case law, the Court derived this requirement from the Constitutional terms "Writings" and "Authors" in the grant of authority to Congress to enact copyright laws.[31]

On the facts before it, the Court held that Rural's white pages telephone directory was uncopyrightable.

> The selection, coordination, and arrangement of Rural's white pages do not satisfy the minimum constitutional standards for copyright protection. . . . Rural's white pages are entirely typical. . . . In preparing its white pages, Rural simply takes the data provided by its subscribers and lists it alphabetically by surname. The end product is a garden-variety white pages directory, devoid of even the slightest trace of creativity.[32]

Rural's selection of listings was "obvious," and its arrangement was "not only unoriginal, it [was] practically inevitable."[33] The Court acknowledged that the telephone white pages were an extreme case, falling in "a narrow category of works in which the creative spark is utterly lacking or so trivial as to be virtually nonexistent."[34] By contrast, it stated, "the vast majority of compilations will pass" the originality test.[35]

Although the holding of *Feist* relates to copyrightability, the Court acknowledged the impact that its reasoning would have on the *scope* of copyright protection for compilations.

---

[30] *Id.* at 346.

[31] *Id.* (quoting U.S. Const., art. I, § 8, cl. 8). The Court hinted, however, that other forms of protection may not be subject to the same constitutional restriction. *See id.* at 354 ("Protection for the fruits of such research . . . may in certain circumstances be available under a theory of unfair competition") (quoting DAVID NIMMER & MELVILLE B. NIMMER, NIMMER ON COPYRIGHT § 3.04 (1990)).

[32] *Id.* at 362.

[33] *Id.* at 362, 363.

[34] *Id.* at 359.

[35] *Id.*

"[C]opyright in a factual compilation is thin. Notwithstanding a valid copyright, a subsequent compiler remains free to use the facts contained in another's publication to aid in preparing a competing work, so long as the competing work does not feature the same selection and arrangement."[36] This represented a complete reversal of the earlier judicial approach in several circuits that held any substantial taking from a copyrightable compilation to be an infringement, and required second-comers independently to collect material for a competing compilation.

C. Subsequent Judicial Interpretation of *Feist*

Feist's teachings have proved important for lower courts both in determining copyrightability and in assessing scope of protection.

1. *Copyrightability*

Subsequent cases have confirmed that the category of works lacking the requisite level of creativity is small. A series of three Second Circuit decisions rendered shortly after *Feist* is illustrative.

In *Key Publications, Inc. v. Chinatown Today Publishing Enterprises Inc.*,[37] the Second Circuit sustained the copyrightability of the yellow pages of a telephone directory for New York's Chinese-American community. The court found that the selection of entries in Key's directory was original.[38] In addition, the arrangement of the directory into categories (e.g., Accountants, Bridal Shops, Shoe Stores, Bean Curd & Bean Sprout Shops) was, when "viewed in the

---

[36] *Id.* at 349. This is consistent with the Court's statement that "[f]acts, whether alone or as part of a compilation, are not original and therefore may not be copyrighted." *Id.* at 350.

[37] 945 F.2d 509 (2d Cir. 1991).

[38] *Id.* at 513.

aggregate," original, because it "entailed the de minimis thought needed to withstand the originality requirement."[39]

In *Kregos v. Associated Press*,[40] the court found the plaintiff's "pitching form" — a form comprised of nine statistics about a pitcher's performance — copyrightable. Kregos' selection of those nine statistics from the universe of statistics that can be used to describe a pitcher's performance could be original, according to the court. Reversing the district court's grant of summary judgment to the defendant, the Second Circuit held that "[i]t cannot be said [as a matter of law that] Kregos has failed to display enough selectivity to satisfy the requirements of originality."[41]

By contrast, in *Victor Lalli Enterprises, Inc. v. Big Red Apple, Inc.*,[42] the Second Circuit found insufficient creativity to support a copyright. The compilation at issue in *Lalli* was comprised of "lucky numbers" used in gambling, arranged in a grid with months along the vertical axis and days of the month along the horizontal axis. The numbers were computed according to a formula that was standard in that industry. The court found no originality in either the selection or arrangement of the data: "Lalli exercises neither selectivity in what he reports nor creativity in how he reports it."[43] The compilation was therefore held uncopyrightable.[44]

---

[39] *Id.* at 514.

[40] 937 F.2d 700 (2d Cir. 1991).

[41] *Id.* at 704.

[42] 936 F.2d 671 (2d Cir. 1991).

[43] *Id.* at 673.

[44] The Sixth Circuit relied on *Victor Lalli* and other cases in concluding that a catalogue of replacement belts "organized in a manner unknown to the industry prior to its publication" was insufficiently creative to qualify for copyright protection. J. Thomas Distribs., Inc. v. Greenline Distribs., Inc., 41 U.S.P.Q.2d 1382 (6th Cir. 1986). There have been a number of recent district court cases addressing the issue of copyrightability as well. *See, e.g.*, Matthew Bender & Co. v. West Pub. Co., 1997 U.S. Dist. LEXIS 6915 (S.D.N.Y. May 19, 1997) (ruling without written opinion that West's pagination of reported cases was not copyrightable, and holding that West's editorial revision of cases themselves entails no copyrightable

Among works that are particularly vulnerable to a finding of uncopyrightability are comprehensive factual databases covering an entire universe of information, where the element of "selection" is lacking and the "arrangement" is obvious.[45] The very comprehensiveness and ease of use of such a database may account both for its commercial value and its lack of protection under copyright.

2. *Scope of Protection*

The *Feist* statement that "the copyright in a factual compilation is thin" has been borne out in case law subsequent to the *Feist* decision. In both *Key Publications* and *Kregos*, the Second Circuit's holding that the work was sufficiently original to be copyrightable was followed by a finding of noninfringement.[46] Although the court had stated in *Key Publications* that, while compilation copyright is thin, "we do not believe it is anorexic,"[47] the scope of protection adopted

---

authorship); Oasis Pub. Co. v. West Pub. Co., 924 F. Supp. 918 (D. Minn. 1996) (upholding copyrightability of arrangement of cases in West's Southern Reporter (relying on West Pub. Co. v. Mead Data Central, Inc., 799 F.2d 1219 (8th Cir. 1986), *cert. denied*, 479 U.S. 1070 (1987)) and finding that defendant's use of star pagination to West page numbers was infringement); National Council on Compensation Ins., Inc. v. Insurance Data Resources, Inc., 40 U.S.P.Q.2d 1362 (S.D. Fla. 1996) (rejecting copyrightability of manual comprised of job codes and formulas used by insurance ratings organization to gather workers' compensation experience data).

[45] *Cf.* Warren Pub., Inc. v. Microdos Data Corp., 115 F.3d 1509 (11th Cir. 1997) (holding plaintiff "did not exercise any creativity or judgment in 'selecting' cable systems to include in its Factbook, but rather included the entire relevant universe known to it"). In spite of the fact that the copyrightability of the plaintiff's compilation was conceded by the defendant (and therefore not an issue on appeal), the court did not find any element of the plaintiff's work that it examined to be protectible. From a plaintiff's standpoint, this has much the same effect as a finding of uncopyrightability, since the only conduct that arguably can be said to infringe is verbatim duplication of the entire work. *See also* American Dental Assoc. v. Delta Dental Plans Assoc., 39 U.S.P.Q.2d 1714 (N.D. Ill. 1996) (selecting dental procedures in "Code on Dental Procedures and Nomenclature" was intended to be comprehensive, and therefore did not exhibit minimal originality to be copyrightable; arrangement of procedures under various headings and subheadings was likewise unoriginal and unprotectible).

[46] The Second Circuit found that the defendant's compilation did not infringe in Key Publications, Inc. v. Chinatown Today Pub. Enters. Inc., 945 F.2d 509, 515-16 (2d Cir. 1991). In Kregos v. Associated Press, the district court reached that conclusion on remand. 795 F. Supp. 1325 (S.D.N.Y. 1992), *aff'd*, 3 F.3d 656 (2d Cir. 1993).

[47] *Key Publications*, 945 F.2d at 514.

in *Kregos* was quite narrow. There, the Second Circuit held that the defendant's compilation would not infringe if it "differs in more than a trivial degree" from the plaintiff's work, essentially creating a "virtual identity" standard for infringement.[48] The Ninth Circuit had also applied a virtual identity standard in compilation cases predating the *Feist* decision.[49] Without necessarily articulating a virtual identity standard, a number of district courts have adopted a similarly narrow scope of protection.[50]

Other courts have accorded even thinner protection to compilations in which copyright was conceded, failing to discern originality in any particular acts of selection or arrangement. In a pair of post-*Feist* cases, the Eleventh Circuit found that copying of significant portions of copyrightable compilations was not infringing because the material copied did not rise to the level of creative authorship.

In *Bellsouth Advertising & Publishing Corp. v. Donnelley Information Publishing, Inc.* ("*BAPCO*"),[51] the Eleventh Circuit held that the defendant's entry into a computer of all of the

---

[48] *Kregos*, 937 F.2d 700, 710; *see also* Harbor Software, Inc. v. Applied Sys., Inc., 936 F. Supp. 167, 170-71 (S.D.N.Y. 1996) (applying "trivial difference test" to screen displays and reports generated by computer program, which court had previously determined to be protectible as compilations).

[49] Harper House, Inc. v. Thomas Nelson, Inc., 889 F.2d 197, 205 (9th Cir. 1989) (treating printed organizer as compilation of uncopyrightable elements and employing virtual identity standard for infringement).

[50] *See, e.g.,* Alexandria Drafting Co. v. Amsterdam, 1997 U.S. Dist. LEXIS 8197 (E.D. Pa. June 4, 1997) (treating plaintiff's maps as compilations of "pictorial facts representing an objective reality," and holding that copying of features such as positions of symbols and street alignments did not constitute infringement); Martindale-Hubbell, Inc. v. Dunhill Int'l List Co., No. 88-6767-CIV-ROETTGER (S.D. Fla. Dec. 30, 1994) (unpublished) (holding that wholesale copying of names, addresses, and other items of information from plaintiff's directory was not infringement). *Cf.* Nester's Map & Guide Corp. v. Hagstrom Map Co., 796 F. Supp. 729, 734 (E.D.N.Y. 1992) (stating that "Key Publications does not stand for the proposition that copying copyrighted materials is proper so long as the copying, though significant, is done in moderation," and finding infringement of plaintiff's compilation of New York City cross streets and building numbers).

[51] 999 F.2d 1436 (11th Cir. 1993) (en banc).

names, addresses and telephone numbers of advertisers in the plaintiff's yellow pages telephone directory, together with business type and type of advertisement, did not infringe.

Since the parties had stipulated to the copyrightability of the plaintiff's directory, and agreed that "the only elements of a work entitled to compilation copyright protection are the selection, arrangement or coordination as they appear in the work as a whole,"[52] the court focused on the elements of selection, coordination and arrangement that the plaintiff claimed were infringed, and found each to be either unprotectible or not copied. For example, the plaintiff claimed (and the district court held) that it selected the listings by determining the geographic scope of the directory, establishing a closing date for changes, and limiting listings to subscribers to its business telephone service, as well as through a variety of marketing techniques. The court found that these elements did not meet the level of creativity required by *Feist*.[53] Moreover, the court did not consider these elements to be "acts of authorship, but techniques for the discovery of facts . . . . The protection of copyright must inhere in a creatively original *selection* of facts to be reported and not in the creative means used to discover those facts."[54]

The court also found the arrangement of the directory "in an alphabetized list of business types, with individual businesses listed in alphabetical order under the applicable headings" to be unoriginal, and to have merged with the idea of a business directory.[55] As to the headings used in the plaintiff's directory, the court did not rule on protectibility, finding as a factual matter that there was insufficient evidence to establish that defendant had copied them.[56]

---

[52] *Id.* at 1438.

[53] *Id.* at 1441.

[54] *Id.* (emphasis in original).

[55] *Id.* at 1442.

[56] *Id.* at 1444. Relying on *BAPCO*, a Florida district court reached the same result in a case involving the Martindale-Hubbell Law Directory. Martindale-Hubbell, Inc. v. Dunhill Int'l List Co., No. 88-6767-DIV-ROETTGER (S.D. Fla. Dec. 30, 1994) (unpublished). The defendant's copying of all of the names

The Eleventh Circuit reached a similar result in *Warren Publishing, Inc. v. Microdos Data Corp.*[57] As in *BAPCO*, the copyrightability of Warren's compilation — a hard copy directory of cable television systems and their owners — was conceded and therefore not an issue before the court.[58] Microdos, the defendant, marketed an electronic database of information on the cable television industry. Warren claimed infringement as to the communities chosen and the designation of certain of them as "lead communities" in circumstances where a cable operator owns systems in multiple communities.[59] The district court had found that "'the selection of . . . communities was creative and protectible because Warren uses a unique system in selecting the communities that will be represented in the Factbook.'"[60] The Eleventh Circuit held that, to the extent that the district court was correct in characterizing Warren's claim as relating to a *system* of selecting communities, section 102(b) of the Copyright Act would bar protection.[61] Even if that characterization were incorrect, the court held that Warren's selection was not original and thus unprotectible. According to the Eleventh Circuit, Warren "did not exercise any creativity or judgment in 'selecting' cable systems to include in its Factbook, but rather included

---

and addresses of lawyers in the plaintiff's directory, together with certain "correlating data" (attorney specialization, title, firm composition and structure) was held not to be an infringement, since those elements were all unprotectible facts. *Id.* at 13-14. As in *BAPCO*, the parties did not dispute the copyrightability of plaintiff's work as a whole. *Id.* at 9.

[57] 115 F.3d 1509 (11th Cir. 1997) (en banc).

[58] *Id.* at 1513 n.4.

[59] *Id.* at 1512. Warren had also claimed infringement as to the data fields and the data field entries. *Id.* The district court found that Microdos had not infringed the data field format and that the data field entries were unprotectible facts. *Id.*

[60] *Id.* at 1516.

[61] *Id.* at 1517. Section 102(b), which is set out in full above, precludes protection for "any idea, procedure, process, system, method of operation, concept, principle, or discovery . . . ." 17 U.S.C. § 102(b).

the entire relevant universe known to it."[62] As to the selection of principal communities, the court held that since Warren made this determination by contacting cable operators and asking them, "the selection is not its own, but rather that of the cable operators."[63] Consequently, the court found no infringement and vacated the district court's injunction.

BAPCO and *Warren* appear to equate a compiler's criteria for selection and organization, respectively, with ideas—which are by definition unprotectible. Taken together, these two cases represent a different approach from the doctrine of "soft facts" or "soft ideas" articulated by the Second Circuit in *CCC Information Servs., Inc. v. Maclean Hunter Market Reports, Inc.*[64] In *CCC*, the Second Circuit posited that there are facts or ideas that are "infused with the author's taste or opinion," as opposed to explaining phenomena or furnishing solutions to problems.[65] The court recognized that using the merger doctrine[66] to rule out protection for the compilation itself by characterizing as "ideas" the criteria used to select or arrange its contents would render copyright for compilations "illusory."[67] This is because "virtually any independent creation of the compiler as to selection, coordination, or arrangement will be designed to add to the usefulness or desirability of his compendium for targeted groups of potential customers, and will represent an idea."[68] The approach taken by the court was, "[i]n cases of wholesale takings of compilations, a

---

[62] *Warren Pub.*, 115 F.3d at 1518.

[63] *Id.* at 1519.

[64] 44 F.3d 61 (2d Cir. 1994).

[65] *Id.* at 71 (relying on *Kregos*, 37 F.2d at 707).

[66] Under the merger doctrine, where an idea can be expressed in only one or a small number of ways, the expression is said to have "merged" with the idea and become unprotectible. *See Kregos,* 937 F.2d at 705; Herbert Rosenthal Jewelry Corp. v. Kalpakian, 446 F.2d 738, 742 (9th Cir. 1971).

[67] *CCC Info. Servs.*, 44 F.3d at 70-71. The court also held that the selection and arrangement of data in a compilation of used car valuations (the "Red Book") "displayed amply sufficient originality" to satisfy *Feist*. *Id.* at 67.

[68] *Id.* at 70.

selective application of the merger doctrine, withholding its application as to soft ideas infused

with taste and opinion . . . "[69]

In summary, very few of the post-*Feist* compilation cases have held entire works to be

uncopyrightable. In fact, copyrightability of the entire work is seldom even contested. Disputes

tend to focus instead on the scope of protection. Consistent with *Feist's* pronouncement that

copyright affords compilations only "thin" protection, most of the post-*Feist* appellate cases have

found wholesale takings from copyrightable compilations to be non-infringing. This trend is

carrying through to district courts as well.[70]

---

[69] *Id.* at 72. *See also* Compaq Computer Corp. v. Procom Tech., Inc., 908 F. Supp. 1409, 1418 (S.D. Tex. 1995) (stating Compaq's compilation of five "threshold values" used to predict imminent failure of disk drive meets *Feist* standard since Compaq made numerous subjective choices requiring creativity and judgment in determining which values to monitor; moreover, "the underlying elements of the compilation are not facts" because they were determined by Compaq based on its estimate of when drive would fail and its business judgment as to when it would be willing to replace it under product warranty); Jane C. Ginsburg, *Copyright, Common Law and Sui Generis Protection of Databases in the U.S. and Abroad*, U. Cin. L. Rev. (forthcoming 1997). *But see* Alexandria Drafting Co. v. Amsterdam, 43 U.S.P.Q.2d 1247 (E.D. Pa. 1997) (copying of "false facts" invented by plaintiff and inserted in its work to detect copying is not infringement); *Nester's Map & Guide Corp.*, 796 F. Supp. at 733.

[70] *See supra* note 51.

18

II. DATABASE INDUSTRY PRACTICES

Many of the issues discussed in this report relate in some way to the manner in which the database industry operates today: how databases are protected against unauthorized use, and how they are licensed. A basic overview of industry practices is useful in examining the adequacy of existing protection and the impact of any changes in the law.

The information in this section is derived from a number of sources, including comments made at the Copyright Office meetings, public documents and submissions prepared by industry members, including a 1995 position paper of the Information Industry Association,[71] informal queries by Copyright Office staff, and third party publications. While details can be difficult to obtain, since database producers are hesitant to make public their proprietary information and business strategies, it is possible to identify certain common or standard practices as well as general trends.

The limitations in the coverage of copyright, described above, have motivated database producers to be creative in protecting their products. They have developed a variety of legal and business strategies, which are typically implemented in combination. In recent years, three main strategies have emerged. Producers have (1) sought to enhance their copyright protection by altering the structure or content of their databases to incorporate greater creativity; (2) increased their reliance on contracts to restrict the use of databases; and (3) employed technological safeguards to prevent unauthorized access and use.[72]

A.   Enhancing Copyright Protection

---

[71] INFORMATION INDUSTRY ASS'N, DATABASE PROTECTION: AN INDUSTRY PERSPECTIVE ON THE ISSUES (1995).

[72] In appropriate circumstances, producers also take steps to secure trade secrecy and trademark protection. As discussed in section VII.B.2-3 *infra*, however, such protection is limited in its applicability.

Some producers have altered the content or structure of their databases, with the goal of obtaining or increasing meaningful copyright protection. One technique is to enhance the contents of the database by adding copyrightable material. Another is to make the database more creative through subjective selection and unusual arrangement of its content. Databases that incorporate one or more of these techniques are often referred to as "value-added databases." While some companies first began enhancing their factual content in response to *Feist*, other companies have built their businesses on this practice for market reasons.

It is difficult to obtain specific examples of "enhanced" databases, since producers do not wish to identify databases that are vulnerable to copying, or point to which aspects of their databases they believe to be copyrightable.

1. *Adding Copyrightable Text*

Some database producers have purposely added copyrightable text to their databases in response to the *Feist* decision. Databases that feature copyrightable text have a stronger likelihood of copyright protection than ones that are purely factual. Such text may take the form of descriptive bibliographies, abstracts, profiles or annotations connected to database entries. A competitor interested in copying only the noncopyrightable portions would face two obstacles: (1) the process of separating facts from text may be labor intensive (though possibly less so as technology improves); and (2) the copyrightable material may be integral enough to give the first producer a competitive edge in the marketplace.

Apart from the copyright implications, a market clearly exists for databases combining text with facts or other public domain materials. EMBASE, for example, is an on-line database from Elsevier Science; its index of titles from international biomedicine, pharmaceutical research and related disciplines includes bibliographic information. American Statistical Index, from Congressional Information Inc., provides abstracts as well as indexing of all federal statistical publications. The reports of judicial opinions published by West Publishing Company include synopses of the cases.

There is a simpler, although less effective, alternative to incorporating copyrightable text throughout the database. Some producers insert text only in designated places, such as the foreword or afterword to a directory, or a section describing community services. As a business matter, such additions may provide consumers with a useful component that other compilations lack. From a legal standpoint, this strategy has limitations. It will make the work as a whole protectible, but will not extend protection to otherwise unprotectible material it contains. It therefore could prevent unsophisticated, verbatim copying, but would not serve as a meaningful barrier to copying of the factual component. The producer will, however, be able to obtain a registration for the database with the Copyright Office. Although the copyright still covers only the copyrightable components of the work, the existence of the registration may deter a would-be copier.

As a variant of this strategy, database producers might insert quasi-factual material such as approximations or "soft facts" into the database. In addition to its utility to consumers, material of this sort may have a greater claim to copyright protection, and may therefore help to ensure copyright protection for the database as a whole.[73] The scope of the protection, however, will remain thin.

2. *Making the Database More Creative*

In the wake of *Feist*, practitioners advised database producers to increase the likelihood of copyright protection by incorporating a more subjective selection of facts or a more creative arrangement.[74] The utility of this strategy depends on the nature of the database. For some databases, such added value may enhance the desirability of the product. Lawyers have long found the West Publishing Company's indexing system of cases by key number to be a valuable

---

[73] *See* discussion of "soft facts" doctrine, *supra,* section I.B.2.

[74] *See, e.g.*, Baila H. Celedonia, *From Copyright to Copycat: Open Season on Data?*, PUB. WKLY., Aug. 16, 1991, at 34 (recommending that compilers "consider enriching their publications in terms of subjective analysis of the[] facts," and attempt to incorporate "value-added subjective selection and arrangement" to make their products more protectible).

research tool. Consumers may prefer a listing of restaurants that weeds out those not worth visiting.

This is not the case, however, for the many databases whose market appeal lies in the availability of comprehensive and easily accessible, unadorned facts. From the point of view of an individual user, added textual information may be superfluous or irrelevant, and may make the database too large or unwieldy. Subjective selection may destroy the database's value as a resource when the user's goal is to examine all the relevant facts. And creative arrangement, to the extent that it is possible,[75] will almost by definition make the facts more difficult to locate. Moreover, adding these elements entails time and money. This may make the database more expensive to create, which in turn may make it more expensive for consumers.

B.   Contractual Protection

For many database producers, contracts provide a major source of protection, either complementing copyright law or picking up the thread where it falls short. Although contracts in the database industry were common prior to *Feist*, in both the digital and the print worlds, companies report that they have reviewed and strengthened them in recent years. These include form contracts as well as negotiated agreements tailored for individuals or institutions. They may appear in traditional print, in shrink-wrap form, on a computer screen as part of software or on-line, or in a combination of these formats. For example, a user may first encounter license terms through shrink-wrap packaging, and then receive the same or additional terms on his computer screen.

1.   Terms of Use

Though terms vary from company to company and from product to product, the core coverage of database contracts tends to be similar: contracts restrict access, specify permissible

---

[75] The contents of a database in electronic form will primarily be arranged by the particular search used to retrieve them, rather than according to an overall, predetermined design of the producer.

conditions of use, and set terms for enforcement and remedies. They may also contain language designed to educate the consumer about legal rights and limitations.

For databases other than those made freely available to the public (such as telephone directories), contracts are generally the condition of access for a user. Even for a noncopyrightable database, they can also offer users the benefit of timely, updated information.[76]

One common use of contracts is to restrict or limit the manner of use of a database. An on-line license typically dictates the parameters of acceptable downloading and redissemination, as in the following excerpts from the agreements of two major database producers, Dun & Bradstreet and Lexis-Nexis:

> You are granted a nonexclusive, nontransferable limited license to access and use for research purposes the Online Services and Materials from time to time made available to you . . . you are prohibited from downloading, storing, reproducing, transmitting, displaying, copying, distributing, or using Materials retrieved from the Online Services. You may not print or download Materials without using the printing or downloading commands of the Online Services.[77]

> Customer shall not . . . use Information in connection with providing advice or recommendations to others, publish Information in the news media, incorporate or use Information in any kind of database or marketing list to be provided to a third party, or produce Information in judicial or administrative proceedings, including discovery proceedings, without D & B's prior written consent, unless required by law.[78]

> Customer shall not copy, download, upload or in any other way reproduce Information or Software except . . . Customer may

---

[76] *See* Ginsburg, *supra* note 70, at 16 ("Copyright is not synonymous with commercial value, and not everything that might be the subject of a license is a subject of copyright. Here, the value is not so much in the content, as in the timing of its delivery. The same stock quote information one hour later is worthless").

[77] Lexis-Nexis Master Agreement, ¶¶ 1.1, 1.3.

[78] Dun & Bradstreet Master Agreement, ¶ 3.3.

create for internal use online and offline printouts of materials received in electronic form.[79]

These agreements limit users' ability to use the contents of databases in ways that the law would otherwise allow.

Other agreements used in connection with databases in CD-ROM format make explicit reference to fair use. For example, a Lexis-Nexis contract for CD-ROMs allows users to "create a printout of an insubstantial portion of material retrieved from the Licensed Databases," and reproduce them "to the extent permitted under the fair use provisions of the Copyright Act."

Contracts may also establish enforcement procedures and remedies. Such terms can include the ability to terminate a subscriber's access, suspend or discontinue services, or pursue any other legal remedy.[80]

Terms may be more restrictive for particularly valuable or sensitive information. Dun & Bradstreet, for example, has strict practices for its sensitive information, such as information relating to bankruptcy filings. For these products, it restricts third party distribution and exercises extreme caution in its licensing practices. By keeping direct control over distribution, the company is always in a position to recall or expand earlier data. It also conducts thorough background checks on potential patrons and extends licenses only to those who are creditworthy and risk-free.

Despite their usefulness, database producers report practical limitations on the effectiveness of contract restrictions, primarily as a result of the privity requirement of contract law.[81] A CD-ROM product, for instance, is physically out of a company's control once delivered to the client. The contract accompanying the product binds only the initial parties; it would not

---

[79] *Id.* at ¶¶ 4.1, 4.2.

[80] *See generally* contracts collected in INFORMATION INDUSTRY ASS'N, CONTRACTS IN THE INFORMATION INDUSTRY III (Peter Marx, ed. 1995).

[81] *See infra* section VII.B.4.

bind third parties who come into possession downstream. As a safeguard, companies may limit CD-ROM licenses to institutions that are not seen as grave risks for piracy.

2.   *Pricing*

As might be expected, different companies provide different types of price structures. Some charge users a flat fee; some charge by byte or by minute for databases made available on-line. Others provide free unlimited access as part of a subscription.

Whatever the system used, it is fairly standard to differentiate prices among users. Companies may offer two-, three-, or even four-tier pricing, contingent on the nature of the use that will be made of the database.[82]   Some do not charge at all for non-profit or academic uses, and then have graduated rates for different commercial uses. In general, commercial producers report that they make their databases available to educational institutions at greatly reduced fees—often a small fraction of the fees to commercial users. Many will charge at least some fee, in order to cover costs, and to make clear that there is value to their product and that it should be treated accordingly.

Recently, educational institutions have tended to seek "buffet-style" terms, allowing unlimited use by as many users as desired for a flat fee. Various mechanisms are utilized, with the fees to such institutions sometimes priced according to the number of users at that institution. A choice of features may also be available, with higher fees charged for better services or software, such as more sophisticated search engines.

In contrast to commercial producers, some science agencies have found price differentiation impractical, since it can be more expensive for them to keep track of who is entitled to which price than to make the information available for free.

---

[82] *See, e.g.,* ProCD, Inc. v. Zeidenberg, 86 F.3d 1447, 1449 (7th Cir. 1996), discussed below in section VII.B.4. ProCD sold its product at one price for consumers and at another, higher price for commercial users. The court noted that this strategy benefited consumers, by providing them a product at an attractive price, as well as commercial users, by allowing ProCD to offer the product to them at a price lower than would be possible in the absence of consumer sales. *Id.*

C.   Technological Safeguards

Technological safeguards, while offering great promise to producers in supplementing legal protection, are still in the early stages of development. Despite the frequent mention of cryptographic software as a technological solution to the protection of intellectual property, such sophisticated protections are not yet in common use. Few if any database producers today rely upon technology as a sole means of protection, utilizing such safeguards only in combination with licensing and enforcement of legal rights.

The technological safeguards in use today are in large part simple, or low-end, measures. Standard measures in the on-line world include the requirement of user-passwords for dial-up services and the ability to disconnect a user whose behavior appears suspect. Lexis-Nexis, for example, will automatically cut off users if contractual limits for downloading are exceeded. In these circumstances, a user's password can be temporarily disabled until further information about his or her actions can be obtained.

Nevertheless, some companies believe that encryption is an option whose time is just around the corner. At present, many users of large databases are institutional clients who obtain access through closed system networks. As more database providers consider making their products available for open exploitation over the Internet by individual consumers, encryption needs will expand. For these providers, the goal is to provide a commercial channel secure enough to allow database content and user payments to be exchanged electronically. They believe the growth of commercial products on the World Wide Web will lead to greater use of access keys and other forms of decryption software. Such options are, in the prediction of one company, a year or so away. For now, the combination of relatively high costs and still undeveloped on-line markets make them impractical. It is likely that any on-line dissemination of databases will involve a combination of encryption, secure electronic transfer of funds, and "click-wrap" licenses requiring users to agree to terms before accessing the database.

Meanwhile, however, a few companies have begun to experiment with encryption for their off-line products. For example, one Dun & Bradstreet product, *Business Solutions in a Box*, is a CD-ROM package of information for small business entrepreneurs. Although the entire database is included on the disk, it appears in encrypted form with restrictions that prevent users from accessing and downloading more than 300 of a possible ten million records unless they pay an additional fee. In keeping with industry trends, however, the encryption is not Dun & Bradstreet's sole protection. Users must assent to these terms in a "click-wrap" license before accessing any of the records.

Database producers consider technological safeguards, like contracts, to be a useful but imperfect solution. Such safeguards cannot protect databases in print form, which still represent a large proportion of the market. Moreover, high-end measures like encryption are, in their current form, expensive to maintain and inconvenient for users. As technology develops, their cost may decrease and their ease of use may increase. Nevertheless, producers report that they will never rely solely on technological measures to protect their products. First, there are security problems. Such measures, like physical locks, can be broken into; encryption keys, for example, can be shared by users in some circumstances.[83] Second, once a database has been lawfully decrypted, the producer cannot control subsequent access to and use of the decrypted version.

---

[83] Security concerns could be ameliorated by legal provisions making it unlawful to circumvent technological safeguards. Such proposals, in the context of safeguards for copyrighted works, are under consideration in Congress as part of implementing legislation for the two World Intellectual Property Organization treaties concluded in Geneva in December 1996 (described *infra* in nn. 175-76). H.R. 2281, 105th Cong., 1st Sess. § 3 (1997); S. 1121, 105th Cong., 1st Sess. § 3 (1997) (adding a new section 1201 to Title 17 that would prohibit "circumvent[ion of] a technological protection measure that effectively controls access to" a copyrighted work).

III. COPYRIGHT OFFICE REGISTRATION PRACTICES

The question of whether and to what extent databases are copyrightable is basic to the discussion of database protection generally and is an underlying theme throughout this report. The Copyright Office, as the agency of the U.S. government responsible for registering copyright claims in works of authorship, makes determinations of copyrightability on a daily basis. Its work includes the task of assessing the copyrightability of databases, which are often dynamic works of authorship and can be fixed in many forms, from print to electronic media. These assessments have important consequences. A registration certificate issued within five years of publication is *prima facie* evidence of copyrightability and of the facts stated in the certificate.[84] Moreover, courts generally give deference to the Register of Copyrights with respect to copyrightability and her decision to allow or deny registration.[85]

Over the years, the Office has developed practices and procedures to assist in determining the copyrightability of the works it examines, including databases. This section discusses registration generally and outlines the practices governing the registration of databases both before and after *Feist*.

---

[84] 17 U.S.C. § 410(c).

[85] *See* Esquire v. Ringer, 591 F.2d 796, 805-06 (D.C. Cir. 1978), *cert. denied*, 440 U.S. 908 (1979) (quoting Bouvé v. Twentieth Century-Fox Film Corp., 122 F.2d 51, 53 (D.C. Cir. 1941)). *Accord*, Custom Chrome, Inc. v. Ringer, 35 U.S.P.Q.2d 1714 (D.D.C. 1995); Jon Woods Fashions, Inc. v. Curran, 8 U.S.P.Q.2d 1870 (S.D.N.Y. 1988); John Muller & Co., Inc. v. New York Arrows Soccer Team, Inc., 802 F.2d 989 (8th Cir. 1986); 1 MELVILLE B. NIMMER & DAVID NIMMER, NIMMER ON COPYRIGHT § 2.08[B][1] (1997) [hereinafter *Nimmer*].

A.   Registration Generally

One of the primary roles of the Copyright Office is to register copyright claims in works of authorship.[86] Although registration is not a condition of copyright protection, it provides many benefits,[87] and is therefore routine practice for many commercial copyright owners, including database producers.

In order to be registered, a work must comprise original authorship. When there is a genuine question about the copyrightability of a work, the Office notes its uncertainty by registering under its "rule of doubt."[88] This means that although the work will be registered, "there is a reasonable doubt about the ultimate action which might be taken under the same circumstances by an appropriate court with respect to whether (1) the material deposited for registration constitutes copyrightable subject matter or (2) the other legal and formal requirements of the statute have been met."[89]

---

[86] 17 U.S.C. §§ 410 and 701(a).

[87] As a practical matter, registration serves as notice to the public that the registrant claims a copyright in the work. The Copyright Act also establishes several incentives for registration. In addition to the evidentiary benefits noted above, better remedies are available for infringement if a work has previously been registered. 17 U.S.C. § 412. *See also* 19 C.F.R. § 133.31(a) (1997) (defining works eligible for recordation with Customs in order to block unauthorized imports as those works which have been registered). Registration is required for a U.S. work in order to sue for infringement, 17 U.S.C. § 411(a), and allows priority in the event of conflicting transfers. 17 U.S.C. § 205.

[88] The "rule of doubt" has never been codified in any version of the Copyright Act, and no court has ruled on its application. It was created by the Copyright Office, which has historically interpreted its responsibilities as permitting discretionary registration in cases of doubt. Herbert A. Howell, former Assistant Register of Copyrights, describing the "rule of doubt," wrote in 1942 that notwithstanding a probable loss of copyright due to failure to satisfy certain complex technical requirements then in effect, "the Copyright Office has always been inclined to give the author the benefit of the doubt, if there be any, and make registration for whatever it may be worth." HERBERT A. HOWELL, THE COPYRIGHT LAW 92 (1942). The Compendium of Copyright Office Practices II directs examiners to register claims in certain factual and legal situations under the rule of doubt, or with a "cautionary" or "warning" letter. *See, e.g.,* Chapter 4 (Notice), § 4.2.4.IV., at 4-29; Chapter 4 (Notice), § 4.3.3.II, at 4-38; Chapter 7 (Works by Foreign Authors), § 7.2.1.II.b, at 7-7; Chapter 8 (Copyright in Works First Published Abroad), § 8.2.1.III.a, at 8-9 [hereinafter *Compendium*].

[89] Compendium § 108.07.

Databases may be collections of works (for example, journal articles) or of data (facts). In examining a database for registrability, the Copyright Office must determine whether it is a protectible "compilation" as defined in the Copyright Act.[90] The Office has prepared guidelines to assist its examiners in determining the copyrightability of databases. General guidelines are set out in the Compendium of Copyright Office Practices.[91] More specific guidelines for databases, including those fixed in automated form, are set out in a series of memoranda issued to the examining staff before and after *Feist* (discussed below).

Where the contents of the database represent new copyrightable subject matter, there is no question that a claim in the database may be registered. Therefore, the Office focuses on whether the claim has been appropriately stated so as to identify that new subject matter. Often, however, the claim is limited to compilation authorship because the contents of the database consist of preexisting materials, whether facts, public domain materials or works that have been previously published. In such cases, the Office must determine whether the selection, coordination or arrangement is copyrightable, making the database registrable.

Where a compilation lacks a certain minimum amount of original authorship, registration will be refused.[92] In general, the greater the amount of material from which to select, coordinate,

---

[90] A compilation is defined in the Copyright Act as "a work formed by the collection and assembling of preexisting materials or of data that are selected, coordinated or arranged in such a way that the resulting work as a whole constitutes an original work of authorship." 17 U.S.C. § 101. *See* discussion of this definition and its meaning *supra* section I.A.

The legislative history of the 1976 Act indicates that compilations can fall within the category of "literary works." H.R. Rep. No. 1476, 94th Cong., 2d Sess. 54 (1976). Most database registration claims are submitted on the form for nondramatic literary works (Form TX). To the extent a database has copyrightable content included in the claim, the nature of the content will usually determine the category of the registration. For example, databases comprised mostly of static graphic images are submitted on the form for "works of the visual arts" (Form VA). Where the authorship in a work falls into more than one category, the appropriate application form is determined by the predominant authorship. 37 C.F.R. § 202.3(b)(2) (1996).

[91] Compendium §§ 307.01, 307.02, 307.03.

[92] *Id.* § 307.01.

or order, the more likely it is that the compilation will be found registrable.[93]   There is also a basic *de minimis* quantity test: "Any compilation consisting of less than four selections is considered to lack the requisite original authorship."[94]

B.   Pre-*Feist* Practices

As a general matter, the Copyright Office has always applied an originality standard in examining works for registration. Until the late 1980's, however, it also registered compilations based on "sweat of the brow."[95] Such compilations included but not were not limited to white pages telephone directories and other factual databases. Beginning in 1987, the Office began to question the copyrightability of works where sweat of the brow was the only basis for registration. By 1989, it had abandoned this standard for most compilations, continuing to apply it only to works like telephone directories in which some courts were still upholding copyrightability based on sweat of brow.

1.   Databases and the Rule of Doubt

Prior to *Feist*, the Office registered a number of compilations under the rule of doubt. The "doubt" was primarily based on the co-existence in case law of the sweat of the brow standard with the 1976 Act's explicit originality standard. One such registration involved the bibliographic database of the On-line Computer Library Center ("OCLC"), which consisted of a collection of numerous member libraries' catalogue entries, where the order was determined by the contributing libraries and the arrangement was chronological. Another case involved an application from the National Republican Congressional Committee for registration of its donor lists, arranged by zip code and alphabetically within each code. The Office registered the list as a compilation, but in

---

[93] *Id.*

[94] *Id.*

[95] *See supra* section I.A.

32

correspondence with the applicant noted its uncertainty and the need for judicial guidance on the copyrightability of compilations of data.[96]

2. *1988 and 1989 Interim Guidelines for Database Registration*

In 1987, the Office reviewed its database practices and considered abandoning its practice of registering sweat of the brow claims. "Interim Guidelines" were issued in 1988 with a memorandum to the staff stating that the courts had concluded that sweat of the brow might still apply to telephone directories but should not be extended to other factual compilations. Examiners were directed to register telephone directories as "a separate category of copyrightable works," and to reject registration for certain other compilations.[97] The Guidelines specified that criteria used to consider the copyrightability of telephone directories should not be applied to other compilations, with the exception of street directories.[98]

Among the types of claims recommended for refusal were 1) in-house directories that contain an entire universe based on a single source arranged mechanically or alphabetically; 2) "parts" catalogues and price lists where the catalogue or update represents an exhaustive list of inventory and the arrangement is numerical; and 3) membership lists containing the entire universe of members arranged alphabetically, by state or zip code.[99] Because these guidelines rejected sweat of the brow as a basis for protection for most categories of work at a time when some

---

[96] In subsequent litigation, the National Republican Congressional Committee filed suit against a private corporation engaged in the commercial sale of various types of data, alleging unauthorized use of its lists. The district court dismissed, finding the copyrightability of the compilation of donor facts incompatible with the public interest goals of the Federal Election Campaign Act; the D.C. Circuit postponed consideration pending a separate, administrative interpretation by the Federal Election Commission. National Republican Congressional Comm. v. Legi-Tech Corp., 795 F.2d 190, 192 (D.C. Cir. 1986). In doing so, the circuit court observed that "the copyrightability of compilations of data is a highly uncertain area of the law which has divided courts and commentators alike." *Id.* at 194.

[97] Memorandum on Copyrightability of Compilations (May 9, 1988).

[98] *Id.* In recognition of the fact that the copyrightability of many compilations would be difficult to judge, the Office made all such rejections subject to supervisory review. *Id.*

[99] *Id.*

jurisdictions still accepted it, there was dissatisfaction with them both in the Copyright Office and within the private sector, and they were never fully implemented.

In 1989, the Office issued "Guidelines for Registration of Fact-Based Compilations." The guidelines advised examiners to register commercial telephone, street and business directories, and parts catalogues and inventory lists that were not "clearly *de minimis*." [100] Examiners were advised to reject standard organization charts and any compilations containing fewer than four items.[101] More difficult claims, such as mailing lists and subscriber lists, were to be rejected unless "the compilation represents a modicum of selection and/or arrangement authorship and the quantity of material compiled is not *de minimis*."[102] The Guidelines stated that telephone directories continued to be treated differently by all federal courts (i.e., even those that otherwise rejected sweat of the brow), and therefore should not be examined under "the usual Copyright Office criteria."[103] Thus, in 1989 the Copyright Office moved almost entirely to an originality standard, rejecting sweat of the brow for all compilations except telephone books and similar directories.

3.   *Registration of Automated Databases*

During the period from 1985 to 1989, the Office considered some special issues posed by automated databases. The Compendium of Copyright Office Practices defines "automated database" as a "body of facts, data, or other information assembled into an organized format, suitable for use in a computer and comprising one or more files."[104]

---

[100] *See* Guidelines for Registration of Fact-Based Compilations at 5-7 (Oct. 10, 1989).

[101] *Id.* at 6.

[102] *Id.* at 7.

[103] *Id.* at 1.

[104] Compendium § 328.

One of the major issues posed by automated databases is the status of ongoing updates or other changes.[105] The Copyright Office has been faced with the need to determine when a modified database qualifies as a new work of authorship subject to a separate registration. To the extent that each update of a database contains copyrightable subject matter, it may be registered.[106] Each registration for a published, updated database covers only the additions that were published on the date specified in the application as the date of publication.[107]

Automated databases may be updated frequently; it is not unusual for a database to be updated several times a day. Database producers on many occasions informed the Office that it was impossible as a practical matter to register and deposit the "new" work each time revisions were made available to the public. Those who did register updated versions adopted certain practices designed to ensure that the bulk of their databases was covered by a registration, generally making regular, but periodic, registrations. OCLC, for example, chose to register its updated database once a month, on a day when many additions and revisions were made. However, because such a registration covered only the new material added on the given date of publication, many published updates and additions were not registered.

To address this problem, in 1989 the Copyright Office adopted a regulation allowing group registration for both published and unpublished automated databases.[108] The regulation

---

[105] In testimony before the Senate Committee on the Judiciary and House Subcommittee on Courts and Intellectual Property in November 1995, the Office took the position that a work is published if copies of the work are electronically transmitted to the public. *See NII Copyright Protection Act of 1995: Joint Hearing on H.R. 2441 and S. 1284 Before the Subcomm. on Courts and Intellectual Property of the House Comm. on the Judiciary and the Senate Comm. on the Judiciary,* 104th Cong., 1st Sess. 42 (1995) (statement of Marybeth Peters, Register of Copyrights). Today, many on-line databases are registered as published; others are registered as unpublished.

[106] *See* 37 C.F.R. § 202.3(b)(4).

[107] U.S. Copyright Office, Circular 65, Copyright Registration for Automated Databases (attached as Appendix A).

[108] *See* 37 C.F.R § 202.3(b)(4) and U.S. Copyright Office Circular 65.

allows three months worth of updates to be registered at one time, with a deposit consisting of identifying material from one representative day.

C.   Post-*Feist* Practices

The *Feist* decision did not have a major impact on the Copyright Office's registration practices for compilations. It did, however, give the Office the clear authority to reject works for which protection was claimed solely on the basis of "industrious collection" or "sweat of the brow."

Immediately following *Feist*, the Copyright Office revisited its examining practices for compilations, and issued new guidelines in 1991.[109] In general, the Office concluded that most compilations would continue to meet the standard of originality required by *Feist*.[110] Nevertheless, examiners were instructed to give extra scrutiny to five types of works: (1) telephone directories; (2) street directories, cross-directories and other directories; (3) periodically updated directories; (4) annual cumulations; and (5) parts catalogues and inventory lists. Specifically, the guidelines advised examiners to reject registration applications where the claim was limited to "white pages," "listings," or "revised listings" in phone books, and to continue to question claims where the nature of the contribution was not clear. More specialized or feature-heavy directories, such as business profiles or annotated membership periodicals, were contrasted as compilations that clearly involve sufficient selectivity to be copyrightable.[111]

In practice, the Office continued to exercise considerable judgment in applying the guidelines. It did not categorically refuse all business directories, for example, registering those it

---

[109] Memorandum from Nancy H. Lawrence, Head, Literary 1 to staff, Literary 1 and 2, Guidelines for Examining Fact-Based Compilations: post-*Feist* (July 8, 1991) [hereinafter *Guidelines*].

[110] *See* Marybeth Peters, *The Copyright Office and Formal Requirements of Registration of Claims to Copyright*, 17 U. DAYTON L. REV. 744 (1992).

[111] Guidelines at 1, 3.

believed to contain copyrightable authorship. The Office sent letters to remitters of compilations, citing the *Feist* holding and the corresponding change in Office practices. In the cases where applicants continued to submit telephone directories, examiners suggested statements of the claim in terms of copyrightable authorship, such as "new text in foreword, " or "revisions and additions to yellow pages."[112] Such correspondence over claim specifications and disclaimers prompted some concern in the private sector that the Office's new practices were akin to a "patentization" of the copyright system.[113]

The Copyright Office's heavy post-*Feist* correspondence lasted for a few months. Within two years of *Feist*, the Office was corresponding with applicants only on occasion. Many applicants sent letters with their submissions, specifying what they believed constituted the originality in their selection, coordination and arrangement.

Despite industry concerns that the Office would interpret *Feist* too broadly, establishing strict bright line rules, the Office continued, and continues today, to accept most compilations submitted for registration. It is impossible to know, however, how many compilation claims are not submitted because their owners are concerned that the Office will question copyrightability or refuse registration.

Occasionally, the Office still receives an application to register white pages telephone directories. In 1991, Southwestern Bell submitted a claim for copyright registration in certain features of the St. Louis White Pages. The company claimed that the work was copyrightable either as a compilation or as a graphic work. The latter claim was based on the typeface and layout of the page, which included various "user-friendly" features. When the Copyright Office

---

[112] *Id.* at 1.

[113] *See, e.g.,* Steven J. Metalitz, *Copyright Registration After Feist: New Rules and New Roles?*, 17 U. DAYTON L. REV. 766 (1992).

denied registration, Southwestern sued under the Administrative Procedures Act.[114] The court

affirmed the Copyright Office's denial of registration, finding no abuse of discretion.[115]

---

[114] *See* 17 U.S.C. § 701(d); 5 U.S.C. §§ 702, 704.

[115] Southwestern Bell Tel. v. Peters, No. 4 Civ. 95CV00886 GFG, at 14, 16 (E.D. Mo. July 31, 1996).

IV. THE INTERNATIONAL CONTEXT

A. International Treaties

Databases have also been the subject of attention in the international arena. Their status as copyrightable subject matter is guaranteed by the two major multilateral treaties relating to copyright. The Berne Convention for the Protection of Literary and Artistic Works since 1948 has required member countries to protect "[c]ollections of literary or artistic works such as encyclopaedias and anthologies which, by reason of the selection and arrangement of their contents, constitute intellectual creations."[116] The coverage of databases of fact was confirmed in 1995 by the TRIPs Agreement,[117] which states: "Compilations of data or other material, whether in machine readable or other form, which by reason of the selection or arrangement of their contents constitute intellectual creations shall be protected as such."[118]

Since January 1996, developed country members of the World Trade Organization have been bound by this obligation; the obligation takes effect for all other members over the next few years.[119] The TRIPs Agreement also specifies that the copyright protection for compilations

---

[116] Berne Convention for the Protection of Literary and Artistic Works, as revised at Paris, art. 2(5) Mar. 1, 1989 [hereinafter *Berne Convention*]. The 1908 revision of the Berne Convention required protection for "collections of different works." Berlin Act, art. 2(2).

[117] Agreement on Trade-Related Aspects of Intellectual Property Rights, 1994, art. 10(2) [hereinafter *TRIPs*]. The TRIPs Agreement constitutes Annex 1C of the Marrakesh Agreement establishing the World Trade Organization (WTO), which was concluded on April 15, 1994, and entered into force on January 1, 1995. TRIPs binds all members of the WTO (*see* art. II.2 of the WTO Agreement).

[118] *Id.* Similar language is contained in the World Intellectual Property Organization (WIPO) Copyright Treaty, Dec. 1996, art. 5 [hereinafter *WIPO Copyright Treaty*] which has not yet become effective. As early as 1982, a meeting of government experts convened by WIPO and UNESCO recognized that "collections and compilations of information" could qualify for copyright protection. *Second Committee of Governmental Experts on Copyright Problems Arising from the Use of Computers for Access to or the Creation of Works* (June 7-11, 1982), *reprinted in* 18 COPYRIGHT 239, 245 (1982).

[119] TRIPs, arts. 65, 66.

"shall not extend to the data or material itself,"[120] and contains another provision stating that "[c]opyright protection shall extend to expressions and not to ideas, procedures, methods of operation or mathematical concepts as such."[121]

B. European Database Directive

1. Background

Pursuant to the action plan set out in its 1991 "Follow-up to the Green Paper,"[122] the European Commission proposed in 1992 to harmonize the national laws within the European Union regarding the protection of databases. The Commission proposal was adopted in a modified form as a directive to the member states on March 11, 1996 (attached to this report as Appendix B).[123] The directive is required to be implemented by the member states by January 1, 1998.

A number of factors appear to have led the European Union (EU)[124] to harmonize the law regarding database protection. The rapid expansion of the Internet raised the EU's awareness of "the exponential growth, in the Community and worldwide, in the amount of information generated and processed annually in all sectors of commerce and industry," and the important role of databases "in the development of an information market within the community."[125] The EU

---

[120] TRIPs, art. 10(2). *See also* WIPO Copyright Treaty, art. 5.

[121] TRIPs, art. 9(2). *See also* WIPO Copyright Treaty, art. 2.

[122] Doc. COM (90) 584 final, 17 Jan. 1991. The "Green Paper" referred to is the 1988 "Green Paper on Copyright and the Challenge of Technology," Doc. COM (88) 172 final, 7 June 1988.

[123] Directive 96/9/EC of the European Parliament and of the Council of the European Union of 11 March 1996 on the legal protection of databases, 1996 O.J. (L 77/20) [hereinafter *Database Directive*].

[124] In this report, for the purpose of simplicity, the European Community and its Member States and the European Union generally are referred to as the "European Union" or "EU."

[125] Database Directive, recitals (10), (9).

also expressed concern about the "very great imbalance in the level of investment in the database sector both as between the Member States and between the Community and the world's largest database-producing third countries."[126] In addition, the *Feist* decision in the U.S. Supreme Court galvanized concern regarding the adequacy of copyright protection for databases within the EU.[127]

The directive covers compilations of data in any form, and thus includes hard copy compilations as well as electronic databases.[128] The Commission's original proposal was limited to electronic databases, but in the course of deliberations this approach was found unworkable, because it would subject the identical material to differing legal standards based solely on the medium employed. As one of the participants is reported to have stated, "making use of a scanner should not be decisive in granting legal protection."[129] In addition, technologies such as scanning and optical character recognition render even hard-copy databases vulnerable to

---

[126] *Id.* recital (11).

[127] Jens-L. Gaster, The New EU Directive Concerning the Legal Protection of Data Bases, *in* FOURTH ANNUAL CONFERENCE ON INTERNATIONAL INTELLECTUAL PROPERTY LAW & POLICY 35, 42 (Fordham Univ. School of Law, Apr. 11, 1996); Mark Powell, The European Database Directive: An International Antidote to the Side-Effects of Feist?, *in* FOURTH ANNUAL CONFERENCE ON INTERNATIONAL INTELLECTUAL PROPERTY LAW & POLICY 49, 57-58 (Fordham Univ. School of Law, Apr. 11, 1996).

[128] Database Directive, art. 1(1), recital (14). The term "database" is defined in the directive as "a collection of independent works, data or other materials arranged in a systematic or methodical way and individually accessible by electronic or other means." Art. 1(2). Explicitly excluded from protection under the directive are "computer programs used in the making or operation of databases accessible by electronic means." Art. 1(3). Recital (17) expands on the definition:

> [T]he term "database" should be understood to include literary, artistic, musical or other collections of works or collections of other material such as texts, sound, images, numbers, facts, and data; . . . it should cover collections of independent works, data or other materials which are systematically or methodically arranged and can be individually accessed; . . . this means that a recording or an audiovisual, cinematographic, literary or musical work as such does not fall within the scope of this Directive.

[129] Gaster, *supra* note 128, at 35, 37. The author, who was the principal administrator within the Commission's copyright unit responsible for the legal protection of databases while the directive was under debate, appears to be quoting or paraphrasing another participant in the discussions.

unauthorized copying and commercial reuse in both hard-copy and electronic form.[130] Moreover, the TRIPs Agreement makes no such distinction.[131]

As adopted, the directive establishes a dual system for protection of databases. One component is copyright protection for the "structure" of the database.[132] The other is a *sui generis* ("of its own kind" — i.e., not falling within existing categories of legal protection) intellectual property right in the contents of the database.

2.   *Copyright Protection*

The copyright portion of the directive, Chapter II, applies only to the structure or schema of a database, without prejudice to any existing protection under copyright for the database contents.[133] It seeks to harmonize the scope of copyright protection for databases throughout the European Union. It does so in two major respects: First, it sets a uniform standard of originality. Second, it establishes a uniform list of "restricted acts" (i.e., exclusive rights) and exceptions to restricted acts.

Prior to the directive, copyright protection for databases in the member states could be divided into two general groups. In the U.K., Ireland and the Netherlands, the threshold for protection was quite low. In particular, Anglo-Irish common law incorporated a "sweat of the brow" doctrine that developed from the same line of eighteenth and nineteenth century English cases that were cited in early U.S. compilation cases.[134] In the remaining European countries, however, copyright imposed a fairly high threshold of originality to qualify for protection.[135] This

---

[130] Powell, *supra* note 128, at 70.

[131] *Id.*

[132] Database Directive, recital 15.

[133] *Id.* art. 3(2).

[134] See discussion, *supra* section I.A.

[135] Gaster, *supra* note 128, at 41-42.

is in keeping with the "author's right" approach that prevails throughout most of Continental Europe, which defines originality as an expression of the author's individual personality.[136]

The standard established by the directive requires the database to, "by reason of the selection or arrangement of [its] contents, constitute the author's own intellectual creation."[137] This language was incorporated verbatim from the EU's 1991 directive on the protection of computer programs.[138] It was originally adopted to override the very high standard of originality mandated by the German Supreme Court in the "Inkasso Programm" case and other decisions.[139] At the same time, by requiring an "intellectual creation," the database directive imposes a higher standard of originality than that required under current law in the U.K., Ireland and the Netherlands. The directive thus charts a middle course on the level of originality required. Although the directive's standard of originality has not been tested in practice, the formulation appears to be quite similar to the criteria for protection under U.S. law, as set out in the definition of "compilation" in the Copyright Act and interpreted by the Supreme Court in *Feist*.[140]

The "restricted acts" (exclusive rights of the copyright owner) under the directive are reproduction (temporary or permanent), adaptation, distribution, and communication, display or performance to the public.[141] Authorization is not required for a lawful user to engage in any

---

[136] Stephen M. Stewart, International Copyright and Neighboring Rights, § 1.13, at 6 (2d ed. 1989). Within this second group of European countries, however, the four Nordic countries (Norway, Sweden, Finland and Denmark) have an additional "related" right for factual compilations, such as catalogues and directories. This "catalogue rule" is discussed *infra* in section IV.B.3.

[137] Database Directive, art. 3(1).

[138] Council Directive 91/250/EEC of 14 May 1991 on the Legal Protection of Computer Programs, 1991 O.J. (L 122/42) [hereinafter *Software Directive*].

[139] Gaster, *supra* note 128, at 39.

[140] *See* discussion *supra* section I.B.

[141] Database Directive, art. 5. The directive only covers economic rights under copyright; moral rights are beyond the scope of the directive. *Id.* recital (28).

43

restricted act "which is necessary for the purposes of access to the contents of the database and normal use of the contents."[142] Any contractual provision to the contrary is "null and void."[143]

In addition to this mandatory exemption, the directive permits member states to provide for limitations on the restricted acts in the following cases:

(a)   in the case of reproduction for private purposes of a non-electronic database;

(b)   where there is use for the sole purpose of illustration for teaching or scientific research, as long as the source is indicated and to the extent justified by the non-commercial purpose to be achieved;

(c)   where there is use for the purposes of public security o[r] for the purposes of an administrative or judicial procedure;

(d)   where other exceptions to copyright which are traditionally authorized under national law are involved, without prejudice to points (a), (b) and (c).[144]

Such exceptions are subject to an overall economic harm limitation, ensuring that they cannot "unreasonably prejudice[ ] the rightholder's legitimate interests or conflict[ ] with normal exploitation of the database."[145]

---

[142] Database Directive, art. 6(1). *Cf.* Software Directive, art. 5(1).

[143] Database Directive, art. 15.

[144] *Id.* art. 6(2). It has been suggested that article 6(2) "narrow[s] the educational and scientific communities' ability to invoke 'fair use' with respect to copyrightable databases under prior law." Jerome H. Reichman & Pamela Samuelson, *Intellectual Property Rights in Data?*, 50 VAND. L. REV. 51, 79 (1997). This view is based on an interpretation of points (a) through (c) as limitations on the scope of any exception permitted under point (d). *Id.* at 77, n.113. Others view point (d) as allowing "other exceptions to copyright which are traditionally permitted by the Member State concerned to continue." Gaster, *supra* note 128, at 40.

[145] Database Directive, art. 6(3). This language is patterned after virtually identical language in the Berne Convention, art. 9(2) and TRIPs, art. 13 (which has been relied on by the United States to permit the doctrine of fair use under copyright law). *See also* WIPO Copyright Treaty, art. 10, and accompanying Agreed Statement (noting the understanding that similar treaty language would "permit Contracting Parties

3. *Sui Generis Protection*

As a supplement to copyright, Chapter III of the directive establishes a *sui generis* form of protection for the contents of databases. The stated justification for this protection is that "in the absence of a harmonized system of unfair-competition legislation or of case-law, other measures are required in addition [to copyright] to prevent the unauthorized extraction and/or re-utilization of the contents of a database," the making of which "requires the investment of considerable human, technical and financial resources while such databases can be copied or accessed at a fraction of the cost needed to design them independently."[146]

Some of the EU member states originally advocated leaving the protection of the contents of databases to unfair competition law, and the initial Commission proposal described the *sui generis* right as a "right to prevent unfair extraction from a database" for commercial purposes.[147] By mid-1993, however, "an increasing majority of interested parties" were reportedly favoring the creation of a property right along the lines ultimately adopted.[148] The rationale, at least in part, was the perceived difficulty in harmonizing unfair competition law throughout the European Union. In addition, the Commission has noted that "unfair competition rules only come into play once an act has taken place. They do not provide an economic right with clear scope which can be freely transferred."[149]

---

to carry forward and appropriately extend into the digital environment limitations and exceptions in their national laws which have been considered acceptable under the Berne Convention.")

[146] Database Directive, recitals (6) and (7).

[147] Proposal for a Council Directive on the Legal Protection of Databases, COM(92)24 final, art. 2 [hereinafter *1992 Proposal*]; *see also* Powell, *supra* note 128, at 68.

[148] Gaster, *supra* note 128, at 42-43.

[149] Submission from the European Community and its Member States to the World Intellectual Property Organization on "An International Treaty on the Protection of Databases," p. 2 (July 1997). For a more complete discussion of the Commission's motivations for abandoning the unfair competition approach, *see* Powell, *supra* note 128, at 62-64 (quoting the Commission's Explanatory Memorandum to the Member States); Gaster, *supra* note 128, at 43 (noting that unfair competition laws apply only to competitive

In some respects the *sui generis* right is similar to the "catalogue rule" existing in the Nordic countries, which provided a model for the Commission. That rule establishes a "related right" for factual compilations, in addition to copyright protection. The catalogue rule provides to the producer of a catalogue, table, or similar matter "in which a large number of information items have been compiled" a right against unauthorized reproduction.[150] Originality is not a requirement for protection, and the term of protection for such "catalogues" is fairly short: 10 years from publication or 15 years from creation, whichever expires sooner.

The essential features of the database directive's *sui generis* right are:

a. **Protection for "substantial investment."** The *sui generis* right is available for "the maker of a database which shows that there has been qualitatively and/or quantitatively a substantial investment in either the obtaining, verification or presentation of the contents . . ."[151] "Substantial investment" is not defined in the directive. However, the recitals leading up to its provisions indicate that "such investment may consist in the deployment of financial resources and/or the expending of time, effort and energy."[152]

b. **Protects against acts of extraction and re-utilization.** The rights accorded under the directive are the rights to "prevent extraction and/or re-utilization of the whole or of a substantial part . . . of the contents of that database."[153] "Extraction" is defined as "the permanent or temporary transfer of all or a substantial part of the contents of a database to another medium

situations).

[150] Swedish Copyright Act, art. 49. *See also* Norwegian Copyright Act, art. 43; Danish Copyright Act, art. 71; Finnish Copyright Act, art. 49.

[151] Database Directive, art. 7(1).

[152] *Id.* recital (40).

[153] *Id.* art. 7(1).

by any means or in any form."[154] "Re-utilization" is defined as "any form of making available to the public all or a substantial part of the contents of a database by the distribution of copies, by renting, by on-line or other forms of transmission."[155]

    c.   **"Insubstantial parts" excluded from protection.** The maker of a database "may not prevent a lawful user of the database from extracting and/or re-utilizing insubstantial parts of its contents . . . for any purposes whatsoever."[156] Any contractual provision to the contrary is "null and void."[157] The directive does not attempt to define "insubstantial parts," but does state that substantiality is to be "evaluated qualitatively and/or quantitatively."[158]

    d.   **Exceptions for certain uses.** The directive permits member states to adopt exceptions from the *sui generis* right for lawful users in three specific categories: (a) extraction for private purposes of the contents of a non-electronic database; (b) "extraction for the purposes of illustration for teaching or scientific research, as long as the source is indicated and to the extent justified by the non-commercial purpose to be achieved"; and (c) "extraction and/or re-utilization for the purposes of public security or an administrative or judicial procedure."[159] These exceptions are similar to those permitted under copyright, but without the additional reference to "other exceptions to copyright which are traditionally authorized under national laws."

---

[154] *Id.* art. 7(2)(a).

[155] *Id.* art 7(2)(b).

[156] *Id.* art. 8(1).

[157] *Id.* art. 15.

[158] *Id.* art. 8(1).

[159] *Id.* art. 9. While not stated explicitly in the text of the provision on exceptions, Recital (50) adds the gloss that the purpose of "such operations . . . must not be commercial."

Nevertheless, the recitals indicate that existing exemptions to any existing similar *sui generis* rights are grandfathered under the directive.[160]

The exceptions must be read in conjunction with provisions in the directive on "obligations of lawful users," prohibiting lawful users of databases that have been made available to the public from "performing acts which conflict with normal exploitation of the database or unreasonably prejudice the legitimate interests of the maker of the database," or "caus[ing] prejudice to the holder of a copyright or related right in respect of the works or subject matter contained in the database."[161]

> e. **Fifteen year term of protection.** The term of protection for the *sui generis* right is fifteen years.[162] This was an increase from the ten-year term that was originally proposed in 1992.[163] Any qualitatively or quantitatively "substantial change," including one resulting from an accumulation of small changes, "which would result in the database being considered to be a substantial new investment," qualifies the resulting database for its own fifteen-year term of protection.[164]

> f. **Available to non-EU nationals only on the basis of reciprocity.** The *sui generis* right is available only to database makers who are EU nationals or habitual residents.[165] For purposes of the directive, this would include business entities that have a business presence in the EU (defined as a central administration or principal place of business in the EU, or a registered

---

[160] *Id.* recital 52.

[161] *Id.* arts. 8(2), 8(3) (again patterned after Berne Convention, art. 9(2) and TRIPs, art. 13). Recital (50) indicates that articles 8(2) and 8(3) function as a limitation on the exceptions in article 9.

[162] *Id.* art. 10(1).

[163] 1992 Proposal, art. 9(3).

[164] Database Directive, art. 10(3). It is unclear whether the new term of protection would apply to the entire database or only the "substantial new investment." Powell, *supra* note 128, at 96.

[165] Database Directive, art. 11(1).

office in the EU plus a genuine, ongoing operational link with the economy of a member state).[166]

The EU can conclude agreements to extend the right to databases made in third countries.[167]

Although the provisions of the directive themselves are silent as to the basis for such agreements,

the recitals make clear that protection will be offered only on the basis of reciprocity— i.e., where

the third country offers "comparable protection" to EU databases.[168]

The original proposal for the directive also included a compulsory license, requiring

database vendors who are the sole source of any given information to license that information to

competitors on "fair and non-discriminatory terms."[169] This provision proved controversial. It

was dropped after the European Court of Justice imposed a similar licensing requirement under

existing principles of EU competition law in the "Magill case."[170] At the same time, apparently as

part of an overall compromise, changes were made in the scope of the right and the exceptions,

as well as the provision on rights of lawful users.[171]

The recitals acknowledge the important role of competition policy in the database area.[172]

In addition, the directive establishes a procedure for review every three years to determine, among

---

[166] *Id.* art. 11(2).

[167] *Id.* art. 11(3).

[168] *Id.* recital (56); Gaster, *supra* note 128, at 46.

[169] 1992 Proposal, art 8(1).

[170] Cases C-241/91 P and C-242/91 P, Radio Telefis Eireann v. Commission of the European Communities, E.C.J. (Apr. 6, 1995) (upholding an order by the Commission requiring television broadcasters to license self-generated programming information to competing publishers of program guides on a non-discriminatory basis).

[171] *See* Gaster, *supra* note 128, at 45.

[172] Database Directive, recital (47) ("Whereas, in the interests of competition between suppliers of information products and services, protection by the *sui generis* right must not be afforded in such a way as to facilitate abuses of a dominant position, in particular as regards the creation and distribution of new products and services which have an intellectual, documentary, technical, economic or commercial added value; whereas, therefore, the provisions of this Directive are without prejudice to the application of Community or national competition rules").

other things, "whether the application of [the *sui generis*] right has led to abuse of a dominant position or other interference with free competition which would justify appropriate measures being taken, including the establishment of non-voluntary licensing arrangements."[173]

4. *Current Status of Implementation*

Member states are obligated to implement the directive by January 1, 1998. Germany has already enacted implementing legislation, and we understand that most of the other member states expect to meet the deadline. All are actively preparing implementing legislation, and several are at an advanced stage in their internal processes of adoption.

C. **Proposed WIPO Treaty**

In February 1996, the European Union submitted a proposal to the World Intellectual Property Organization (WIPO) in Geneva for a treaty on the subject of legal protection for databases, for consideration by the WIPO Committees of Experts that had been meeting on a regular basis to discuss two other proposed treaties in the field of copyright and neighboring rights.[174] The European treaty proposal would have required countries adhering to the treaty to establish a new, non-copyright form of protection for databases, referred to as *sui generis* protection. It was based on essentially the same concept contained in the directive, but framed in the simpler, more bare-bones style of international treaty language. The European proposal was distributed and briefly discussed at the Committee of Experts meeting that took place the week of February 5-9.

---

[173] *Id.*, art. 16 (3).

[174] These two treaties, which had been under discussion for several years, were intended to update and improve on existing international standards of protection in the area of copyright and neighboring rights. The current forms of the major WIPO treaties in this area, the Berne Convention for the Protection of Literary and Artistic Works, and the International Convention for the Protection of Performers, Producers of Phonograms and Broadcasting Organizations (the "Rome Convention"), date back to 1971 and 1961, respectively.

The next Committee of Experts meeting took place in May 1996. For consideration at that meeting, the United States submitted its own treaty proposal on the subject of database protection. This proposal differed from that submitted by the EU in several respects, primarily relating to the protectibility of government databases (the U.S. proposed allowing countries to deny protection), the term of protection (the U.S. proposed 25 years), the requirements for protecting foreign databases (the U.S. proposed national, i.e. non-discriminatory, treatment), and the ability to vary rights by contract (the U.S. proposed complete freedom of contract). Again, there was a brief debate of the database issues, during the course of a week-long discussion including the two other proposed treaties. The meeting concluded with a decision by the Committees to recommend to the Governing Bodies of WIPO that a Diplomatic Conference be convened in December 1996 to consider the adoption of treaties in all three areas.

On August 30, 1996, WIPO distributed draft texts of three treaties prepared by the Chairman of the Committees of Experts, Jukka Liedes of Finland, based on the various treaty proposals made by governments and the Committees of Experts' discussions of those proposals. One of the three, entitled "Basic Proposal for the Substantive Provisions of the Treaty on Intellectual Property in Respect of Databases to be Considered by the Diplomatic Conference" (the " Draft Database Treaty" or "draft treaty"), dealt with the proposed *sui generis* right in databases.[175] A copy is attached as Appendix C.

The draft treaty combined elements of both the European and the U.S. proposals. As is standard in WIPO treaties, it set out the basic concepts of the subject matter of protection and the

---

[175] The other two drafts were the Basic Proposal for the Substantive Provisions of the Treaty on Certain Questions Concerning the Protection of Literary and Artistic Works to be Considered by the Diplomatic Conference, WIPO Doc. No. CRNR/DC/4 (Aug. 30, 1996), and the Basic Proposal for the Substantive Provisions of the Treaty for the Protection of the Rights of Performers and Producers of Phonograms to be Considered by the Diplomatic Conference, WIPO Doc. No. CRNR/DC/5 (Aug. 30, 1996). Both were negotiated and ultimately adopted, although in substantially different form, by the WIPO Diplomatic Conference in Geneva in December 1996. *See* WIPO Copyright Treaty and World Intellectual Property Organization Performances and Phonograms Treaty, Dec. 1996 [hereinafter *WIPO Performances and Phonograms Treaty*].

nature and duration of the rights, but left to individual countries the freedom to flesh out the details through exceptions and limitations.

The draft was structured as follows: A preamble described the importance of databases in the global information infrastructure and the need to provide effective legal protection for them on an international basis. Article 1 set out the scope of protection, requiring contracting parties to protect databases in any form or medium, based on the criterion of "a substantial investment in the collection, assembly, verification, organization or presentation" of the contents, irrespective of any protection under copyright or other legal rights in the database under national law.

The rights to be granted were defined in Article 3 as "the right to authorize or prohibit the extraction or utilization" of the database's contents. They were to be granted to the maker of the database, and thereafter be freely transferable.[176] No formalities could be imposed on the enjoyment and exercise of the rights.[177]

Article 2 contained definitions of the critical concepts of "database," "maker of the database," and "substantial investment," as well as the acts of "extraction" and "utilization" that constituted the rights to be granted, and the term "substantial part" appearing in the definition of those acts. "Database" was defined as "a collection of independent works, data or other materials arranged in a systematic or methodical way and capable of being individually accessed by electronic or other means." The "maker of the database" was "the natural or legal person or persons with control and responsibility for the undertaking of a substantial investment in making a database." The requisite "substantial investment" was defined as "any qualitatively or quantitatively significant investment of human, financial, technical or other resources in the collection, assembly, verification, organization or presentation of the contents of the database."

---

[176] Draft Database Treaty, art. 4.

[177] *Id.* art. 9.

An act of "extraction" was "the permanent or temporary transfer of all or a substantial part of the contents of a database to another medium by any means or in any form," while an act of "utilization" was

> the making available to the public of all or a substantial part of the contents of a database by any means, including by the distribution of copies, by renting, or by on-line or other forms of transmission, including making the same available to the public at a place and at a time individually chosen by each member of the public.

Finally, the "substantial part" referred to in both of these definitions was itself defined as "any portion of the database, including an accumulation of small portions, that is of qualitative or quantitative significance to [its] value."

Exceptions were dealt with in Article 5. Using the long-accepted language from the Berne Convention[178] and the TRIPs Agreement,[179] this article allowed individual countries to provide exceptions or limitations to rights "in certain special cases that do not conflict with the normal exploitation of the database and do not unreasonably prejudice the legitimate interests of the rightholder." It also left to national determination the treatment of databases made by governmental entities, agents or employees.

Two alternatives were given for the term of protection: either 15 or 25 years.[180] A separate paragraph required a new term of protection when a database is changed through a new investment sufficient to qualify for protection in itself:

> Any substantial change to the database, evaluated qualitatively or quantitatively, including any substantial change resulting from the accumulation of successive additions, deletions, verifications, modifications in organization or presentation, or other alterations, which constitute a new substantial investment, shall qualify the

---

[178] Berne Convention, art. 9(2).

[179] TRIPs, art. 13.

[180] Draft Database Treaty, art. 8.

53

database resulting from such investment for its own term of protection.[181]

This term of protection would apply not only to databases produced after the entry into force of the treaty, but also those that were already in existence at that time.[182] The resulting new protection for existing databases would not affect, however, any "acts concluded or rights acquired" before the treaty's entry into force, and countries could allow continued distribution of previously lawfully made copies for a period of up to two years.

The draft treaty made clear that the new form of protection would not affect in any way other laws relating to databases or their contents, including copyright, antitrust law, data protection and privacy, access to public documents and the law of contract.[183]

Each country would be required to protect makers of databases who were nationals of other contracting parties, on a national treatment basis—i.e., providing the same rights in respect to *sui generis* protection that it provided to its own nationals.[184] Finally, the draft contained the same provisions on technological protection measures and enforcement of rights as were contained in the two other draft treaties.[185]

The treaty proposal proved controversial within the United States. Numerous comments were submitted to the Patent and Trademark Office, with the overwhelming majority opposing conclusion of a treaty at that time, expressing concerns about the impact of such protection and/or urging delay until there had been an opportunity for full domestic debate. This group of

---

[181] *Id.* art. 8(3).

[182] *Id.* art. 11.

[183] *Id.* art. 12.

[184] *Id.* arts. 6-7.

[185] *Id.* arts. 10 and 13. *See* Basic Proposal on a Treaty on Certain Questions Concerning the Protection of Literary and Artistic Works, arts. 13 and 16; Basic Proposal on a Treaty for the Protection of the Rights of Performers and Producers of Phonograms, arts. 22 and 27. (In the final, adopted treaties, different versions of these provisions became articles 11 and 14, and 18 and 23, respectively.)

commentators included members of the scientific, library and educational communities, as well as individual members of the public and at least one major database producer. Those commenting in favor were companies and trade associations from the publishing and database industries.

The draft treaty on databases was never reached or discussed in substance at the December 1996 Diplomatic Conference. The negotiation of the other two treaties continued throughout the entire three weeks of the Conference, concluding only in its final hours on the last day. During the Conference, a number of delegations expressed the view that the database treaty was premature, and that they were not ready to negotiate its provisions. Ultimately, the Conference adopted a recommendation that the Governing Bodies of WIPO should convene in March of 1997 and decide on the course of future work on the issue.

On March 20-21, the Governing Bodies determined that the subject of legal protection for databases should be taken up again in a meeting in Geneva on September 17-19, 1997. This will be an informational meeting, where delegations will discuss the treatment of databases under the laws of their respective countries, and their experiences in dealing with the subject. The draft treaty itself is not scheduled to be the topic of debate.

V. PRIOR CONGRESSIONAL CONSIDERATION

During 1996, the possibility of legislation providing a new form of protection for databases was raised in the respective Congressional committees dealing with intellectual property.

In February 1996, the chief intellectual property counsel for the Senate Committee on the Judiciary attended the meeting of the WIPO Committees of Experts in Geneva, and reported to the delegates that the Senate was examining the issue and considering the introduction of legislation.

On May 23, 1996, during the next WIPO Committees of Experts meeting, Congressman Carlos Moorhead, then Chairman of the House of Representatives Subcommittee on Courts and Intellectual Property, introduced H.R. 3531, entitled the "Database Investment and Intellectual Property Antipiracy Act of 1996" (attached as Appendix D).[186] Like the subsequently-prepared WIPO draft treaty, the bill would have protected databases that result from a substantial investment against various acts of unauthorized extraction or use. As is usual with national legislation, the bill differed from the treaty primarily in containing more detail, particularly about the scope of rights and exceptions, as well as in spelling out remedies.

Section 2 was the definitional section. It defined "database" as "a collection, assembly or compilation, in any form or medium now or later known or developed, of works, data or other materials, arranged in a systematic or methodical way." The terms later relied on to delineate the prohibited acts, "extraction" and "use and reuse," were defined as follows:

> "Extraction" means the permanent or temporary transfer of all or a substantial part of the contents of a database or of a copy or copies thereof. Such transfer may be to an identical or different medium, and by any means or in any form, now or later known or developed.

---

[186] H.R. 3531, 104th Cong., 2d Sess. (1996) [hereinafter *H.R. 3531*].

> "Use" and "reuse" means making available all or a substantial part, qualitatively or quantitatively, of the contents of a database, or access to all or such substantial part, whether or not for direct or indirect commercial advantage or financial gain, by any means now known or later developed, including any of the following: (i) marketing, selling, or renting; (ii) in the form of permanent or temporary copies; or (iii) by distribution, any online or other form of transmission.

The bill did not define "substantial part," but defined its opposite, "insubstantial part," as "any portion of the contents of a database whose extraction, use or reuse does not diminish the value of the database, conflict with a normal exploitation of the database or adversely affect the actual or potential market for the database."

Section 3 set out the standards a database would have to meet to qualify for protection. A database would qualify

> if it is the result of a qualitatively or quantitatively substantial investment of human, technical, financial or other resources in the collection, assembly, verification, organization or presentation of the database contents, and (i) the database is used or reused in commerce; or (ii) the database owner intends to use or reuse the database in commerce.[187]

Specifically excluded from protection were databases made by a governmental entity, whether state or federal, but not databases whose contents were obtained from such an entity.[188] Another subsection ruled out protection for computer programs.[189]

The prohibited acts were set out in Section 4. The bill would have made it unlawful to perform the following acts without authorization:

> (1) extract, use or reuse all or a substantial part, qualitatively or quantitatively, of the contents of a [protected] database . . . in a manner that conflicts with the database owner's normal exploitation

---

[187] *Id.* § 3(a).

[188] *Id.* § 3(c) and definition of "Governmental entity" in § 2.

[189] *Id.* § 3(d).

of the database or adversely affects the actual or potential market for the database;

(2) engage . . . in the repeated or systematic extraction, use or reuse of insubstantial parts, qualitatively or quantitatively, of the contents of a [protected] database . . . in a manner that cumulatively conflicts with the database owner's normal exploitation of the database or adversely affects the actual or potential market for the database; or

(3) procure, direct or commission any [of the foregoing] act[s].[190]

The bill further provided examples of circumstances in which acts of extraction, use or reuse *would* be considered to conflict with a normal exploitation of the database or adversely affect its actual or potential market.[191]

Exceptions were dealt with in Section 5. One paragraph stated that a lawful user of a database could extract or use insubstantial parts of its contents for any purpose, subject to the "repeated or systematic" test of section 4(2), set out above.[192] The other made explicit that anyone was free independently to collect, assemble or compile from other sources any of the material contained in a database.[193]

Section 6 established the duration of protection. It provided a basic term of protection of 25 years, but with the ability to obtain a new term upon "any change of commercial significance."

Sections 7 and 8 established remedies, both civil and criminal.

---

[190] *Id.* § 4(a).

[191] *Id.* § 4(b) (these circumstances involved direct or indirect competition in the database's current market or one which its owner had a "demonstrable interest or expectation" in entering; uses aimed at reasonably likely customers for the database; or multiple users within an organization without a license covering them).

[192] *Id.* § 5(a).

[193] *Id.* § 5(b).

Section 9 explained the relationship of the proposed protection to other bodies of law. It stated that copyright protection would not be affected, and that parties would remain free to enter into contractual agreements with respect to databases or their contents.[194] It also made clear that

> [n]othing in th[e] Act shall prejudice provisions concerning copyright, rights related to copyright or any other rights or obligations in the database or its contents, including laws in respect of patent, trademark, design rights, antitrust or competition, trade secrets, data protection and privacy, access to public documents, and the law of contract.[195]

Sections 10-13 dealt with the circumvention of technology used to protect databases against unauthorized acts, and with the integrity of database management information. Their language paralleled similar prohibitions contained in the then-pending bills proposing a National Information Infrastructure Copyright Protection Act.[196]

Section 14 contained a three-year statute of limitations.

Section 15 made the date of enactment the effective date of the act, and barred liability for the use or reuse of database contents lawfully extracted from a database prior to that date.

The House bill was introduced as an indication to the international community that Congress was interested in pursuing the subject of database protection. No hearings were held, and no corresponding bill was introduced in the Senate.

---

[194] *Id.* §§ 9(a) and (b).

[195] *Id.* § 9(c).

[196] H.R. 2441, 104th Cong., 1st Sess. § 4 (1995); S. 1284, 104th Cong., 1st Sess. § 4 (1995).

In the months following introduction of H.R. 3531, many of the groups that had opposed conclusion of the draft WIPO treaty expressed similar concerns about the bill relating both to substance and to timing and process. They urged that all interested parties be given an opportunity to provide input and that a thorough analysis of the issues be undertaken. Their substantive concerns are reflected in the discussion of the issues in Section VII below.

VI. COPYRIGHT OFFICE MEETINGS

A.   Procedure

In order to provide Congress with complete and balanced information, the Copyright Office sought to meet with as many interested parties as possible. The Office initiated the process by scheduling a series of five meetings with the major groups that had already been vocal in indicating their interest in the subject of database protection: (1) the library community; (2) science agencies and organizations; (3) educational groups; (4) database producers who favor legislation; and (5) database producers who oppose legislation or do not favor it at this time. The goal was to start by ascertaining the shared views and concerns of each of these identifiable groups.

These meetings took place in March, May and June of this year. The participants were selected as follows: the Office identified those entities and individuals whose interest we had learned of through prior contacts and discussions. We added the names of organizations and associations who had submitted comments to the Patent and Trademark Office on the WIPO draft database treaty, or who had contacted the staff of the Congressional committees to communicate their concerns. We then asked representatives from each group to suggest any additional parties who should be invited. Finally, some participants contacted us directly with requests to attend.

Subsequent meetings were scheduled with persons or entities whose interests were distinct from the larger groups, or who had scheduling problems making it difficult for them to attend the large meetings. The Office also met with several academics and lawyers with particular expertise on the subject, who shared their own analysis of the issues presented. Finally, we made ourselves available to meet with anyone else who wished to communicate views or concerns. In total, the Office held sixteen meetings, as well as receiving a number of additional communications, including by mail or telephone.

The meetings were structured to provide an informal environment conducive to focused, productive and open discussion. All were led by Marybeth Peters, the Register of Copyrights, with the assistance of the staff of the Office of Policy and International Affairs. Each participant was given an opportunity to present its specific views, and then an unlimited time period was devoted to general discussion of the issues. While there were no formal presentations or questions, Copyright Office staff occasionally asked questions to clarify facts or positions. The discussions were not transcribed, and written statements were not required, although some participants chose to submit them during or after the meetings.

A list of those attending the meetings is attached to this report as Appendix E. We note that the number of participants on any side of an issue was purely the result of the selection process described above. The Office made no attempt to achieve a numerical balance or to evaluate the relative size or importance of any interest group or position.

B.   Overview of Positions

This section gives a general overview of the views expressed in the Copyright Office meetings. Inevitably, it cannot constitute a complete or perfectly accurate description of any one party's or group's views, but represents our best effort at communicating the essence of each position. There will, of course, be numerous opportunities at later stages in the process of legislative consideration for additional presentations and submission of materials. We do not identify particular parties, except where necessary to describe a distinct point of view.

From the outset, the Copyright Office made clear that it was starting from first principles and working from a clean slate, rather than assuming that any of the proposals from last year would be the starting point for Congressional consideration. During the meetings, however, elements of prior proposals were frequently discussed, and these discussions are reflected below where useful and relevant.

The meetings indicated that core elements of agreement exist as to certain principles, where the difficulty lies primarily in determining how to implement those principles (whether by legislation or the absence of legislation). Thus, participants generally agreed on the following points: (1) databases are vulnerable to copying, and adequate incentives are needed to ensure their continued creation; (2) individual facts should not be the subject of private ownership; (3) anyone should be free to obtain facts independently from original sources, even after they have been incorporated in a database; (4) government databases should not be protected; (5) it is important not to harm science, research, education and news reporting; and (6) "free riding" in the form of substantial copying for commercial, competitive purposes should not be permitted.

In other areas, there is intense disagreement as to fundamental principles. The participants sharply differed, for example, on the adequacy of existing means of protection for databases; whether additional statutory protection or its absence is more likely to diminish access to data or raise its cost; and whether non-competitive uses that may harm the market for a database should be permitted.

Some participants in the Copyright Office meetings held strong views either in favor of new legislation or in opposition. In general, many members of the library and scientific communities, as well as some educational groups, telephone companies and Internet-related businesses, expressed opposition, while a majority of database producers, including producers of a variety of scientific and scholarly databases, and the owner of a major on-line retrieval service advocated legislation. It must be stressed, however, that positions were not uniform within all of these communities. Some commercial database producers, including one of the largest in the global marketplace, oppose legislation at this time; many scientific researchers, particularly those working for industry, favor it. The reasons for the differences among those who appear to be similarly situated were not always clear. In some cases, it may simply be that they hold differing perceptions of the law or the potential dangers posed.

A large number of the participants were undecided, or took neutral or intermediate positions. Many have interests on both sides of the issue, as they both produce databases and rely on information obtained from the databases of others. They generally expressed a desire to ensure adequate incentives, along with concerns about the possible negative impact of new protection. For some of these participants, their view of any legislation would turn on the form and scope of protection it provided. Others were still analyzing the issues, and had not yet formed an opinion.

The Office also met with several groups or entities with no position on the advisability of legislation generally, but with a specific concern about how some aspect of any such legislation might affect their activities. Most of these participants stated that if a need were established for new protection, and it was possible to provide adequate protection without harming legitimate user interests, they would either support or not oppose legislation.

This section briefly summarizes the positions of those with clear views either pro or con. More detail will be given in the discussion of the issues below.

Proponents

Proponents of new legislation make the following principal points:

(1) Databases are increasingly important to the U.S. economy and to science, and will be a key component of content on the Internet. They often provide information not otherwise available from a single source in a usable form, and ensure that the information is reliable and timely. Given the acceleration of developments in communications, storage and retrieval technologies over the past five to ten years, vast quantities of information are made available today much more quickly, and users have much greater capabilities to access and manipulate it. In addition, markets and science have evolved to demand increasing levels of comprehensiveness, accuracy and timeliness.

(2) Large investments of time and money are necessary to produce and maintain many databases. Voluminous information must be collected, placed in a usable format, and kept accurate and up-to-date.

(3) While it is expensive to collect and verify large numbers of facts, it is increasingly cheap to copy and disseminate them. Databases are therefore vulnerable to acts of piracy that threaten to destroy or significantly reduce their markets. This threat has been growing with the evolution of technology. With today's digital and scanning capabilities, major investments in both online and hard copy databases can be hijacked with the stroke of a key.

(4) Existing law is insufficient to protect against this threat. Although various forms of protection are available today, both legal and technological, there has been a gap in the law since the Supreme Court's decision in *Feist Publications v. Rural Telephone Service Co.*, resulting in an inability to obtain satisfactory legal relief in many circumstances. Problems have already been experienced by a number of database producers. It is critical to restore the protection against piracy that existed under the "sweat of the brow" theory of copyright law.

(5) Unless adequate protection is available for databases that require substantial resources to produce and maintain, such investments will significantly diminish. The result will be a loss not only of commercial profits, but of the public benefits accruing from the creation of databases and access to the information they contain. On the international level, markets for databases have become global, and the United States must provide adequate protection if it is to avoid competitive disadvantage with other regions of the world such as the European Union.

(6) The needed protection can be provided through appropriately crafted new legislation without harming the legitimate interests of the science community and other user groups. Indeed, scientific research will benefit from such protection, since researchers rely heavily on the private sector to make the high levels of investment necessary to produce and maintain reliable, up-to-date and comprehensive collections of scientific data.

Opponents

Generally, those that oppose new protection or are doubtful about its advisability do not contest the proponents' assertions as to the importance of databases, the changes brought about in their creation, dissemination and use by developments in technologies, and the need to provide adequate incentives. They disagree as to the conclusions to be drawn, however, and make the following points:

(1) Proponents have not produced sufficient evidence that a problem exists that requires a legislative solution. Their arguments about the need for additional protection are based on theory, isolated anecdotes, and speculation about possible future harm. International developments, particularly the outcome of the European directive, will not cause them serious detriment. It would be premature for Congress to legislate without more extensive factual evidence, or without expert economic analysis.

(2) The combination of means of protection that exist today appears to be adequate. Copyright law continues to protect databases even after *Feist*. The Supreme Court in *Feist* explicitly stated that most databases would still qualify for copyright protection, and subsequent cases have borne this out. Moreover, recent case law has made clear that meaningful protection is available outside of copyright through contract and the common law of misappropriation. Technological means of protection are also available and effective. Proponents can come to Congress if this situation changes, for example if the case law begins to develop in an unsatisfactory direction.

(3) The U.S. database industry today is an example of market success, not market failure. The industry is thriving under the current legal regime, and has become the leader in the global marketplace. Databases continue to be created and marketed, and businesses are paying record sums of money to purchase database producers.

(4) In this area, it is critical to proceed with great caution, especially in a time of rapidly evolving technologies and uses of data, since it is hard to predict future implications. New protection could result in negative consequences, even if unintended. A perceived trend toward

commercialization of data, particularly data produced by government funding, could be exacerbated. Information could as a practical matter become less accessible or more expensive; concern about potential liability could have a chilling effect on uses of information that are in the public interest, such as scientific research and education. New legal protection could raise a new barrier to market entry for second comers, decreasing rather than increasing already low levels of competition and driving up prices.

(5) Copyright law embodies an appropriate balance between incentives for creation and the free flow of information, by granting rights but leaving ideas and facts in the public domain and providing leeway for public interest activities through the doctrine of fair use and other exceptions. This balance furthers Constitutional policies and should not lightly be disturbed. New rights should not be provided, especially if they give equivalent or greater protection than copyright, without the justification of creativity; facts should be left free for all to use.

In addition to these general points, government science agencies have raised concerns about the impact of any new protection in this area on the policy of full and open access to data that the United States has strongly pursued in the international arena.[197]

---

[197] *See generally* COMMITTEE ON ISSUES IN THE TRANSBORDER FLOW OF SCIENTIFIC DATA, U.S. NATIONAL COMMITTEE FOR CODATA, AND NATIONAL RESEARCH COUNCIL, BITS OF POWER: ISSUES IN GLOBAL ACCESS TO SCIENTIFIC DATA (1997); discussion *infra,* section VII.B.7.

VII. ISSUES

A.   General

During the course of the meetings, several key issues began to emerge. At each meeting, different ones were stressed, different concerns expressed, and different subsidiary issues identified. Overall, however, most of the substance of the discussions can helpfully be grouped under one of six topics. It should be noted that the issues are interrelated in many respects, so that they cannot each be resolved in a vacuum.

The first, and threshold question, is whether additional legal protection for databases is needed. Several participants made the point that even if a need were shown for additional protection, Congress should not enact legislation without performing a cost-benefit analysis to determine whether the need outweighed the harm that would be caused by any such legislation. Of course, the ultimate test of any proposed legislation is whether its benefits outweigh its costs, and this test would have to be met in order for any form of database protection to be enacted. We have not addressed it as a separate issue in the report, however, because the question of what harm might be caused is dependent on how all of the other issues are resolved. Accordingly, our discussions of potential harm occur in the context of specific issues. For example, certain types of harm might be avoided by adopting certain exceptions, or otherwise framing the scope of protection in a certain way.

If the threshold question of need is answered in the affirmative, the next question is what type of protection would be preferable—a new form of property right, or a tort concept closer to unfair competition. The remaining issues also would only need to be addressed if Congress decides that some form of legislation is desirable. These are: (1) definitional issues—how should the concept of "database" be defined, what should be the criteria for a database to qualify for protection, and what degree of taking should be actionable? (2) how can it be ensured that uses of information in the public interest, such as for scientific, educational and news reporting

71

purposes, are not harmed? (3) what should be the duration of any such new protection? and (4) how should "sole source" data be handled—i.e., situations where the data contained in a protected database is not available elsewhere? One additional issue was not discussed at any length in the meetings, but would need to be examined: what constitutional constraints may limit Congress's ability to legislate in this area. We discuss each of these issues in turn, describing the main points raised in the meetings.[198] In the process, we note those points where the issues are most obviously inter-related.

B.   Is There a Need for Additional Protection?

All agree that the proponents of a new form of statutory protection have the burden of establishing the need for such protection. Some participants in the Copyright Office process chose to refrain from discussing any other issue pending the resolution of this first issue. They felt that they could not analyze what models of protection might be appropriate before identifying clearly the nature and scope of the problem.

Establishing such a need is the threshold question for any legislative initiative. Traditionally, the proponent of any change in the law, whether new rights or new limitations on rights, has borne the burden of convincing Congress of the need for the change.

Views diverge sharply, however, as to the type and degree of proof required to satisfy this burden. The options proposed ranged the gamut from a threat of future harm, to evidence of individual real-world problems, to empirical data generated through broad-scale studies. In the past, changes in intellectual property law have often been based on evidence of one of the first two types. Those arguing for economic studies believe that a higher standard is necessary here,

---

[198] On any particular issue, the description of one side's views may be significantly longer than the description of another side's. This does not mean that the Copyright Office ascribes greater weight to those views or believes they are more persuasive, simply that one side raised more numerous or more complex points.

either because it is preferable for the establishment of any new right, or because of the special nature of protection for collections of data in particular.

Various forms of protection against piracy do exist today for databases in the United States. Chief among these are copyright law, contracts, state misappropriation doctrine, trade secrecy, trademark law, and technological means of protection. The question is whether the combination of these existing sources of protection is sufficient to provide adequate incentives to produce a suitably wide variety of databases.

Much of the time at the meetings was devoted to debating this question. The remainder of this section summarizes the arguments on both sides.

1. *General*

Proponents argue that existing forms of protection are not sufficient. Some forms protect only certain limited aspects of databases, insufficient to reward the investment required to produce them; others are not well-defined and established, or uniform in geographic application. They perceive a gap in protection since the Supreme Court in *Feist* ruled out copyright for the "sweat of the brow" involved in producing a database, and believe that gap has had real-world negative consequences. They argue that Congress should stay ahead of the curve and prevent more serious harm from occurring.

In particular, proponents describe several cases where database producers have been unable to obtain relief from the courts against substantial, competitive copying.[199] The economic significance of such losses, they assert, has been evidenced by the effect on the producers' stock prices.[200] They report that piracy has been a problem for others as well, but has not yet led to

---

[199] *See, e.g.*, Warren Pub., Inc. v. Microdos Data Corp., 43 U.S.P.Q.2d 1065 (11th Cir. 1997); Matthew Bender and Co., Inc. v. West Pub. Co., 42 U.S.P.Q.2d 1930 (S.D.N.Y. 1997); Skinder-Strauss Assoc. v. Mass. Continuing Legal Educ., Inc., 914 F. Supp. 665 (D. Mass. 1995); Martindale-Hubbell, Inc. v. Dunhill Int'l. List Co., No. 88-6767-CIV.- ROETTGER (S.D. Fla. Dec. 30, 1994).

[200] *See, e.g.*, Raymond Snoddy, *Reed Elsevier Shares Drop on U.S. Legal Ruling*, FIN. TIMES, May 23, 1997.

litigation. They express an understandable reluctance, however, to draw attention to particular databases as possibly uncopyrightable or subject to thin protection.

In addition, proponents assert that uncertainties in U.S. law have begun to affect investment decisions, with producers choosing not to create particularly vulnerable databases, or not to disseminate them broadly, because of a perception that the risks are too great. At least some large database producers in the United States and some European producers have reportedly been unwilling to make their databases available on-line in this country, despite the potential for substantial profit from that form of exploitation. One producer has even decided not to make its print database available to libraries because of a fear of piracy by library patrons.

Opponents, in contrast, view such evidence as insufficient, either because it is isolated, or because it is based on speculation as to future harm. They believe that existing law is adequate, and that the courts are generally drawing appropriate lines between protection and free use. Moreover, they point out that legal protection can be supplemented by technological protection, and argue that database producers should avail themselves fully of their existing options before seeking a legislative solution.

2. *Copyright*

As discussed in section I above, databases are copyrightable subject matter under U.S. law. Proponents value the benefits of copyright protection, and rely on it to the extent possible, but point out that copyright provides only limited protection for databases. While most databases remain copyrightable after *Feist* (and indeed the Court was careful to state that the white pages directory before it represented an extreme case),[201] it is precisely those databases that require the greatest amount of investment and may be the most valuable to users whose copyright status is most doubtful: the massive, comprehensive database covering the entire universe of a given field, produced in electronic form with the arrangement of the data not fixed by the producer but

---

[201] *Feist*, 499 U.S. at 359.

chosen by each individual user. For such databases, it may be difficult for a court to discern any acts of selection or arrangement on the part of the compiler rising to the level of creative authorship.

One rational response of database producers to *Feist*'s analysis has been to add as many copyrightable elements as feasible to their databases (whether additional text or creative methods of selection or arrangement).[202] The result of such changes or additions may be to make the information in the databases less easily accessible to users, or less complete. As the capabilities of personal computers and mass marketed software such as search engines increase, consumers are more and more interested in products that offer comprehensive raw data in electronic form for their own selection and arrangement.

A database of meteorological, environmental or medical information, for example, must be comprehensive, accurate, and up-to-date, or the results could be injurious to health or safety. And it is most useful when organized in the most logical, obvious way possible. Subjective selection or a unique arrangement may impede the database's utility or ease of access. Even where this is not the result, resources are diverted from the task of collecting and disseminating information to the task of satisfying copyrightability thresholds—a diversion that may not be in the best interests of the public, as it is likely to lead to less production of content or higher prices.

At least of equal concern to proponents is the question of the scope of protection for copyrightable databases. In *Feist*, the Supreme Court made clear that the copyright in a compilation is "thin"—that it will not prevent the copying even of all the material contained in the compilation, if the copier does not take the creative elements of selection, coordination or arrangement that made the compilation copyrightable.[203] In other words, if the copyright in a

---

[202] *See* discussion *supra* section II.

[203] *Feist*, 499 U.S. at 349.

database is based solely on its unusual arrangement of the data, a competitor may download and reuse all of the data that was collected at great expense, as long as the format is different.

Judicial developments since *Feist* have augmented rather than allayed these parties' concerns about the adequacy of copyright protection for databases. They read many of the subsequent cases as applying *Feist*'s teachings broadly, resulting in an extremely narrow and almost meaningless scope of protection. These cases, they say, hold that very little in any database is protectible, and that virtually everything of value is free for the taking. In particular, they point to the decisions in *BAPCO v. Donnelley* and *Warren Publishing*, discussed above in Section I.B., both of which allowed commercial competitors to extract substantial amounts of the contents of expensive-to-produce databases, finding that various acts of selection and arrangement did not meet *Feist*'s standard of minimal creativity.

Opponents believe that existing copyright law is adequate and appropriate, as supplemented by the other forms of protection described below. While they focused more on other issues during the meetings, some stressed the fact that very few databases have been held unprotectible, and viewed the thin scope of protection provided by the courts to be appropriate in light of the public interest in access to information.

3.   *Trade Secrets*

While not discussed much at the meetings, trade secrecy law may also provide protection to certain databases. Compilations of data are one of the types of material that can be protected as trade secrets.[204] Several of the necessary elements of a trade secrecy claim, however, make such a claim unlikely for the typical database. First, the data must not be common knowledge, and must have been kept secret. Disclosure through sale, display, or circulation of goods embodying the compilation, for example, will forfeit trade secret status.[205] As a result, only those

---

[204] Restatement of Torts § 757 comment b (1939); Restatement (Third) of Unfair Competition § 39 comment d (1993).

[205] 1 ROGER M. MILGRIM, MILGRIM ON TRADE SECRETS § 105[2] (1996) [hereinafter *Milgrim*].

databases produced for internal use, and not made available to the public or exploited commercially, will be eligible for protection. Second, a claim for breach of trade secrecy requires a relationship between the owner of the secret and the defendant, involving either a contract or a confidential relationship,[206] or the use of improper means such as theft, fraud, or inducement of breach of confidence.[207] The ordinary act of use or exploitation of a database would otherwise not be covered.

4.   *Trademark*

Some protection may also be available for databases under trademark law. For those databases that have come to be identified with a particular producer, the unauthorized use of material from the database in a manner that creates a likelihood of confusion as to source may be actionable under state or federal trademark law.[208] This can be important, especially for databases with users like scientists who rely on the names of reputable publishers in determining the reliability and timeliness of data.

Proponents point out, however, that such protection is limited; it will primarily be of assistance for famous "brand name" databases, such as Dun & Bradstreet's credit reports. Moreover, it will only protect against those uses of the database that involve the trademark and confuse the consumer as to the database's origin.

---

[206] *Id.* at § 3.03.

[207] 2 Milgrim § 7.03; Restatement (Third) of Unfair Competition § 43 (1993).

[208] *See generally* J. THOMAS MCCARTHY, TRADEMARKS AND UNFAIR COMPETITION § 23 (1996) [hereinafter *McCarthy*]; 15 U.S.C. § 1125(a) (Lanham Act § 43(a)). The related doctrine of dilution may also provide limited protection against certain unauthorized uses of a producer's trademark. Under federal law, a use of a mark that lessens the "capacity of a famous mark to identify and distinguish goods or services" is unlawful. 15 U.S.C. §§ 1125(c)(1), 1127 (definition of "dilution"). *See also* McCarthy § 24.14 (discussing state anti-dilution statutes).

5. *Contracts*

As discussed in section II.A.2 above, database producers are increasingly relying on contractual restrictions to protect their databases against unauthorized use. So far, such contracts have generally survived claims of invalidity based on state contract doctrines such as contracts of adhesion[209] and on preemption by copyright law. The most authoritative and well-known opinion to date is *ProCD v. Zeidenberg*, [210] which held valid and enforceable a shrinkwrap license barring unauthorized commercial uses of a computer program and database, rejecting the argument that a contract preventing unauthorized use of data was preempted by the Copyright Act.

Some have described contractual protection as the most flexible and effective form of legal protection available for databases, since it allows producers to tailor the permissible conditions of use in a manner appropriate to the particular type of database and the particular type of user. For example, as in *ProCD* itself, a producer may adopt a two-tier system of distribution, offering the database at a low price for consumer or non-profit uses, and charging substantially more for commercial uses. Similarly, more restrictive terms can be used for particularly valuable or sensitive items in a database, such as credit ratings.[211]

Proponents of new legislation agree that contractual protection is an important source of protection for databases. They give a number of reasons, however, why they do not believe it is sufficient.

---

[209] *But see* Vault Corp. v. Quaid Software Ltd., 847 F.2d 255, 269 (5th Cir. 1988) (affirming district court holding that shrink-wrap software license was a "contract of adhesion" unenforceable under Louisiana law absent a preempted state statute); Shoptalk Ltd. v. Concorde-New Horizons Corp., 897 F. Supp. 144 (S.D.N.Y. 1995) (declining to enforce contractual obligation to pay royalties after the expiration of the copyright in the work for which they were paid).

[210] 86 F.3d 1447 (7th Cir. 1996).

[211] *See* discussion *supra* section II.A.2.b.

First is the privity problem: contracts bind only those in privity, not unrelated third parties.[212] So while a contract may suffice to block unwanted activity by the immediate customer, it may not prevent such activity by downstream users. If, for example, a CD-ROM originally sold with a shrink-wrap license is dropped on the street, the person who finds it may place its contents on the Internet without contract liability. Contract protection therefore appears to work particularly well for databases with a limited group of customers that have an ongoing relationship with the database producer. It may be less satisfactory for databases that are sold in hard copy form or marketed through multiple levels of distribution.

A second concern relates to enforcement. The remedies available for breach of contract differ in various respects from those provided by the Copyright Act. Most important is the fact that specific enforcement of a contract is rarely available,[213] whereas injunctive relief is standard in copyright cases and operative throughout the country.[214] In addition, plaintiffs in breach of contract actions must prove damages,[215] whereas copyright law provides statutory damages and the possibility of an award of costs and attorney's fees to the prevailing party.[216]

Moreover, contractual protection is a creature of state law only. As a consequence, the law may vary from state to state, with a contract that is effective in one state potentially

---

[212] *See ProCD*, 86 F.3d at 1454 (stating that contracts "generally affect only their parties"); Wilde v. First Federal Sav. & Loan Ass'n, 134 Ill. App. 3d 722, 731, 480 N.E.2d 1236, 1242 (1985) (validly formed contract held not enforceable against one who is not in privity).

[213] *See* E. ALLEN FARNSWORTH, FARNSWORTH ON CONTRACTS §§ 12.4-12.6 (1990) (Supp. 1996) (stating that courts historically have been unwilling to compel performance of contract if legal remedy of damages is adequate to protect injured party).

[214] 17 U.S.C. § 502.

[215] *See* Restatement (Second) of Contracts § 352 (1981); Uniform Commercial Code (U.C.C.) § 1-106 comment 1; U.C.C. § 2-715 comment 4; Farnsworth, *supra* note 214, at §§ 12.8-12.9.

[216] The Act permits statutory damages "in a sum of not less than $500 or more than $20,000 as the court considers just," and up to $100,000 in the court's discretion for willful infringement. 17 U.S.C. § 504(c). Costs and attorney's fees may be awarded to the prevailing party in the court's discretion. 17 U.S.C. § 505.

unenforceable in another. The *ProCD* case itself was based on a federal appeals court's reading of the Wisconsin Uniform Commercial Code.[217]

A related jurisdictional issue raised by proponents is that even if state contract law is relatively consistent, many databases are marketed on a global scale. The contract laws of other countries tend to diverge more widely from the standard U.S. model, sometimes placing greater restrictions on freedom of contract based on each country's conceptions of public policy.[218]

In addition, the enforceability of such contracts is not well settled, and has generated controversy. The *ProCD* case is the view of a single court of appeals, and may not prove to be the ultimate judicial word on the subject. Meanwhile, the ongoing project for the reform of the Uniform Commercial Code, administered by the American Law Institute (ALI) and the National Conference of Commissioners on Uniform State Laws (NCCUSL), includes a proposed Article 2B which would govern transactions in software and licenses in information. "Information" is defined to include data, databases, and "any intellectual property or other rights in information."[219] The issue of whether and to what extent such contracts can provide protection for data, or vary exceptions and limitations contained in the Copyright Act, is under debate.[220]

---

[217] ProCD, Inc. v. Zeidenberg, 908 F. Supp. 640, 651 (W.D. Wisc. 1996), *rev'd*, 86 F.3d (7th Cir. 1996). Although the license for a shrink-wrapped consumer item was held to be governed by U.C.C. art. 2 (sales), courts may not necessarily apply the U.C.C. to other licenses.

[218] *See, e.g.,* Turner Entertainment Co. v. Huston, Court of Appeal of Versailles [France], Combined Civil Chambers, Decision No. 68, Roll No. 615/92 (Dec. 19, 1994) (as translated in 16 Ent. L. Rep. (March 1995)) (declining to enforce employment contract between U.S film studio and U.S. director and screenwriter due to French public policy favoring moral rights). *See also* 1 MELVILLE B. NIMMER AND PAUL EDWARD GELLER, INTERNATIONAL COPYRIGHT LAW AND PRACTICE 198-99 (1993) (discussing enforcement of employment "work for hire" agreements outside United States generally).

[219] Article 2B-102(19) (May 5, 1997 Draft). *See generally* Raymond T. Nimmer, *Issues: Meeting the Information Age* (May 3, 1996) <http://www.law.uh.edu/ucc/2b>.

[220] On May 19, 1997, ALI adopted an amendment to the current draft of section 2B-308, which deals with mass market licenses. The amendment reads: "In mass-market licenses, a term that is inconsistent with applicable provisions of the copyright law cannot become part of a contract" under the mass-market section. Transcript, ALI Annual Meeting (May 19, 1997), pp. 33-34. An earlier version of the amendment specifically prohibited terms that are inconsistent with section 102(b) of the Copyright Act, the codification

Finally, the argument has been made that contractual protection may not be optimal from the consumer's point of view. If relegated entirely to contractual self-help, database producers may make their products available only on license terms that are more restrictive than the terms that would be set by federal law. Such a trend may be developing already today, as some producers respond to their insecurity about legal protection after *Feist* by making databases available only with shrinkwrap licenses or on proprietary networks, and only upon terms barring many otherwise permissible uses.[221]

Opponents question the seriousness of the privity problem. They assert that the chief value of many databases lies in their constant updating—especially those comprehensive databases that may not meet *Feist's* creativity standard, and tend by their nature to be dynamic. If the producer of such a database suspects leakage, it can cut off access to the offending customer and block the current information flow that makes the database valuable.

In general, opponents stress that the law so far has confirmed the effectiveness of contractual means of protection, and that contracts today are relied on by many database producers. If the law should develop in a different direction, Congress could then consider the issue.

6. *Misappropriation*

Another existing form of protection for databases is provided by state common law under theories of misappropriation. The seminal case in this area dates back to 1918, when the Supreme Court held that the Associated Press (AP) had a claim against the International News Service

---

of the idea/expression dichotomy. If adopted into state law, this amendment might be read to overrule *ProCD*'s holding on this point and make it impossible for database producers to rely on contracts to limit the use of data in their databases.

On July 29, however, NCCUSL adopted a motion stating its belief that article 2B should not address the subject of this amendment, "but should adopt a position of neutrality on the issues which are being actively debated at federal and international levels," and suggested that ALI revisit its position.

[221] *See supra* section II.B.

(INS) to prevent it from copying news items from the war front gathered by AP at great trouble and expense, and scooping AP by making the items available to INS subscriber newspapers for advance publication.[222]

Although the *INS* decision was based on no-longer extant federal common law,[223] it has been relied on over the years by various state courts in fashioning relief for similar conduct.[224] *INS* was cited by the Supreme Court several times in the 1980s and '90s, including in *Feist*.[225] Congress also referred to it in fashioning the preemption provision of the 1976 Copyright Act.[226]

---

[222] International News Serv. v. Associated Press, 248 U.S. 215 (1918).

[223] *See* Erie R.R. v. Tompkins, 304 U.S. 64, 78 (1938).

[224] *See generally* Douglas G. Baird, *Common Law Intellectual Property and the Legacy of International News Serv. v. Associated Press,* 50 U. CHI. L. REV. 411 (1983).

[225] *See Feist*, 499 U.S. at 354 (stating that legal protection for facts "may in certain circumstances be available under theory of unfair competition"); Carpenter v. United States, 484 U.S. 19, 26 (1987); San Francisco Arts & Athletics v. United States Olympic Comm., 483 U.S. 522, 532 (1987).

[226] 17 U.S.C. § 301. *See* H.R. Rep. No. 1476, 94th Cong., 2d Sess. 132 (1976); S. Rep. No. 473, 94th Cong., 2d Sess. 116 (1976). The reference reads in full:

> "Misappropriation" is not necessarily synonymous with copyright infringement, and thus a cause of action labeled as "misappropriation" is not preempted if it is in fact based neither on a right within the general scope of copyright as specified by section 106 nor on a right equivalent thereto. For example, state law should have the flexibility to afford a remedy (under traditional principles of equity) against a consistent pattern of unauthorized appropriation by a competitor of the facts (i.e., not the literary expression) constituting "hot" news, whether in the traditional mold of *International News Service v. Associated Press*, 248 U.S. 215 (1918), or in the newer form of data updates from scientific, business, or financial data bases. Likewise, a person having no trust or other relationship with the proprietor of a computerized data base should not be immunized from sanctions against electronically or cryptographically breaching the proprietor's security arrangements and accessing the proprietor's data. The unauthorized data access which should be remediable might also be achieved by the intentional interception of data transmissions by wire, microwave or laser transmissions, or by the common unintentional means of "crossed" telephone lines occasioned by errors in switching.
>
> The proprietor of data displayed on the cathode ray tube of a computer terminal should be afforded protection against unauthorized printouts by third parties (with or without improper access), even if the data are not copyrightable . . .

The doctrine remained, however, somewhat ill-defined and uncertain in scope, as different courts applied it in different circumstances, sometimes without refined analysis.[227]

The misappropriation doctrine gained renewed clarity and authority earlier this year, when the Second Circuit decided *National Basketball Association v. Motorola, Inc.*[228] In holding that a narrow form of common law misappropriation was not preempted by the Copyright Act, the Second Circuit delineated the elements of the surviving claim, and explained how it differed from copyright. According to the court, protection would be available under New York common law, without preemption, in the following circumstances:

> (i) a plaintiff generates or gathers information at a cost; (ii) the information is time-sensitive; (iii) a defendant's use of the information constitutes free-riding on the plaintiff's efforts; (iv) the defendant is in direct competition with a product or service offered by the plaintiff; and (v) the ability of other parties to free-ride on the efforts of the plaintiff or others would so reduce the incentive to produce the product or service that its existence or quality would be substantially threatened.[229]

In the case before it, the court held that the National Basketball Association did not have a cause of action because it failed to show free-riding by the defendants or a sufficient competitive effect on the markets for its own products.[230]

Again, those seeking new federal protection acknowledge that the misappropriation doctrine is useful, but assert that it is insufficient for several reasons. First, they identify several potential shortcomings of the doctrine as elucidated by the Second Circuit. Whether or not the result in *Motorola* is appropriate, the court's analysis establishes the "hotness" or timeliness of the

---

[227] *See, e.g.*, Metropolitan Opera Assoc., Inc. v. Wagner-Nichols Recorder Corp., 101 N.Y.S.2d 483 (Sup. Ct. 1950), *aff'd*, 279 App. Div. 63, 107 N.Y.S.2d 795 (1951).

[228] 105 F.3d 841 (2d Cir. 1997).

[229] *Id.* at 845.

[230] *Id.* at 853-54.

data as a necessary element; apart from the question of how hot is "hot," the value of many investment-rich databases may lie in the comprehensiveness of the collection of historical or timeless information. They also note that the commercial value of a database may be significantly harmed by unauthorized uses made by parties that are not in direct commercial competition, such as multiple uses by a member of the database's intended audience or use by a commercial entity in preparing a related but distinct type of database. As under copyright law, they argue that the database producer should be able to protect its ability to exploit potential markets as well as those already being utilized.[231] Finally, the fifth element, relating to the reduction of incentives to produce, has been criticized as relating more to the degree of damage suffered by the database producer than to the nature of the wrongdoing.

More generally, proponents express concern that the tort of misappropriation is not well-defined or established in every state, and therefore leaves unclear where databases are protected and to what extent. The *Motorola* case is one decision in one Circuit, applying the law of one state; other state laws may be interpreted differently, and other courts may rule differently on the preemption issue. Proponents believe that both greater certainty and national uniformity are necessary for meaningful protection in today's marketplace, especially in the on-line world. With inconsistent approaches in different states, difficult issues of choice of law and jurisdiction are likely to arise. These concerns are magnified in the international context.

Opponents of new protection view the misappropriation doctrine as a strong and effective means of protection, targeting with some precision the type of conduct most likely to cause meaningful commercial harm, while avoiding an impact on beneficial, public interest types of uses. As to the specific critiques of the doctrine described above, some argue that the "hotness" of the data is a reasonable criterion for protection, given the economic value of timely updates and the negatives to be weighed in the balance in protecting information. They also argue that as a policy

---

[231] *Cf.* 17 U.S.C. § 107(4) (in determining fair use, courts are to take into account effect of use on work's potential market).

matter, limiting the legal claim to directly competitive markets is preferable, in order to avoid chilling the development of new, collateral database products. Competitors could then freely use information for different purposes, such as developing specialized niche databases. Or an entrepreneur could analyze historical financial data from the stock exchanges in order to predict future trends for investors.

As to the question of common law versus federal legislation, opponents assert that the courts are so far doing a reasonable job of interpreting and applying the doctrine of misappropriation. They urge that Congress should not step in prematurely where there does not yet appear to be a problem, but rather let the common law continue to develop. Some suggest that, if necessary, Congress instead consider amending section 301 of the Copyright Act to make clear that misappropriation claims are not preempted.

7. *Technological Protection*

In the increasingly important on-line environment, database publishers, like other creators of intangible materials, are looking to technological means to protect their products against unauthorized use. More and more sophisticated and effective forms are being developed today. Both owners and users cite such technological measures as critical elements of a workable system of protection, and at least a partial answer to the question of how to deal with the increased vulnerability to piracy in a digital world.

To proponents, such technological means of protection are necessary but not sufficient. The arguments made on both sides generally mirror the arguments that are made in the copyright context. On the one hand, technological protection has the potential to be extremely effective, easier and more economical to rely on than legal rights, and could obviate as a practical matter the need for additional legal protection; on the other hand, such protection is still in developmental stages, can be defeated by technological means of circumvention, does not prevent use of the database once someone has obtained an authorized copy in accessible form, and is effective primarily for databases in electronic form.

85

Some express concerns that technological protection could be <u>too</u> strong, making database producers completely invulnerable. They fear that producers, able to control every use made on-line, will impose stricter limits and permit less fair use.

8. *International Considerations*

One final aspect of the asserted need for new legislation is an outgrowth of the larger international context. Proponents point out that the market for databases, especially large and investment-intensive electronic databases, is global in scale. Accordingly, they are concerned not only about the level of protection in the United States, but in other countries as well.

In particular, they point to developments in Europe, where the recent directive on legal protection for databases effectively conditions protection for non-European Union databases on reciprocal protection in the given database's country of origin. In other words, an American database generally will not receive *sui generis* protection in EU member states unless U.S. law provides similar protection to databases.

Proponents argue that as of the beginning of 1998, when the directive's requirements take effect, American database producers will therefore be at a competitive disadvantage in Europe, one of the biggest markets for such works, as compared to their European counterparts. The latter will be able to control and profit from the use of their products, while the American producers will not. Related risks to market share are that U.S. producers will need to adopt more restrictive and less user-friendly contracts than their foreign competitors, and will not be able to operate safely in those jurisdictions where on-line or shrink-wrap contracts may not be respected. Concern is also expressed as to the effect on other countries outside the European Union of a failure to provide statutory protection in the United States, particularly those countries where piracy of U.S. works is a major problem today.

If, on the other hand, American database producers choose to avail themselves of the directive's alternate route to protection by establishing a commercial presence within the

European Union, proponents argue that the result will be a loss of jobs in the United States, with a corresponding detriment to the U.S. economy.

Opponents state that the United States should not follow Europe unless it is convinced that the European approach is a good idea. Rather, the United States should take the lead in establishing appropriate intellectual property policy, and seek to persuade the European Union and others to adopt our approach. This is particularly true, they argue, in areas relating to the use of government data, where the U.S. approach has historically differed from that of many European nations. There has long been controversy between the United States and Europe over appropriate treatment of such data, with the United States championing a policy of full and open access.[232]

Some opponents are concerned about potential negative international implications from enactment of new protection. They agree that markets are international in scope. Scientific research in particular increasingly involves international collaboration and the sharing of data collected globally. Several countries may participate in producing and maintaining a database, such as the database of DNA sequencing information created by the U.S., Japan and Europe. Research today requires the use of data sets from around the world. Science agencies caution that the United States should not send the wrong signal to other countries, and risk encouraging

---

[232] The U.S. government has been engaged for several years in espousing international agreements regarding full and open access to data. A multilateral policy to this effect was recently adopted in the World Meteorological Organization (WMO), with member countries agreeing to provide free and unrestricted exchange of meteorological and related data. WMO Policy and Practice for the Exchange of Meteorological and Related Data and Products Including Guidelines on Relationships in Commercial Meteorological Activities (WMO Resolution 40 (Cg-XII)) (1995). Numerous policy statements from international organizations and conferences, including the United Nations and the Organization for Economic Cooperation and Development, affirm this same goal in the context of other scientific disciplines as well.

governments to allow control of access to information, especially in a time of increasing budgetary constraints and corresponding commercialization of scientific data.[233]

Moreover, opponents express doubt that all member states of the European Union will have *sui generis* legislation in place by 1998, and believe it is uncertain what form such legislation might take. Even assuming the directive is fully implemented, they question whether it creates a real need for action. They assert that U.S. database producers will be no worse off in Europe than they are today, when *sui generis* protection does not exist, since they will merely fail to obtain the benefit of an *added* level of protection.[234] They also point out that some U.S. producers already qualify for protection under the directive because they have a place of business in a member state, and those that do not can simply establish one.

Opponents question predictions of a meaningful competitive disadvantage. Rather, they believe any advantage to European producers will be only marginal. If a significant problem does arise, they argue, Congress can then respond.

Finally, opponents suggest that the directive's failure to provide national treatment may be challenged as an impermissible trade practice, inconsistent with existing treaty obligations, or as an inappropriate approach to intellectual property in a global marketplace.

C.   Form of Any New Protection

If Congress determines that a need has been established for additional protection, the next question is what form that protection should take. Two basic models have been proposed, both in

---

[233] Past proposals in the United States have made clear that there would be no protection for government data.. *See* H.R. 3531 § 3(c). Other countries, however, might choose to proceed differently (as they have in the area of copyright). *See, e.g.*, Hong Kong Copyright Ordinance, Ord. No. 92 of 1997 §§ 182-186 (1997); United Kingdom Copyrights, Designs and Patents Act of 1988 §§ 163-167 (1988).

[234] While the Directive will lower the level of copyright protection in some member states, it will raise the level in others. *See* discussion *supra* section IV.B. Accordingly, if *sui generis* protection is not provided to U.S. database producers in the European Union, they are likely to have less protection than today in some places and more in others.

the United States and in the course of debate over the directive in the European Union: (1) an exclusive property right; or (2) some form of unfair competition law, focusing on the nature of the conduct prohibited rather than providing ownership rights in particular subject matter.

The final version of the European directive adopts an exclusive property right model, as did the treaty proposals put on the table in WIPO last year and, at least arguably, the bill introduced in the 104th Congress. These approaches all provided database makers with certain specified rights in defined subject matter, lasting for a set period of time, transferable by contract, and subject to potential exceptions and limitations.

In contrast, an unfair competition model would not confer rights owned and enforceable against the world, but would make it unlawful to engage in conduct identified in some way as unfair.[235] It would be closer to concepts contained in the Lanham Act, and embodied in the misappropriation doctrine set out in the *INS* and *Motorola* cases.

A federal misappropriation statute need not adopt every element of the state law claim outlined in *Motorola*, however, or in the same way. In the context of federal legislation, those elements that may be necessary to avoid preemption are not necessarily required, since in this context Congress itself would be determining where to draw the line between protection and free use. The issues would rather be the sufficiency of coverage of such legislation, and its compatibility with any constraints imposed by the Constitution.[236]

The choice between the two models has many potential ramifications. Depending on how it is drafted, an unfair competition model could obviate the need for definitions, for exceptions, or for a defined term of protection. The international consequences could also be quite different; in

---

[235] Arguably, unfair competition principles were the true basis of the pre-*Feist* sweat of the brow directory cases. Commentators have noted the "reaping where one has not sown" language and rationale of many of the opinions. *See, e.g.,* Jane C. Ginsburg, *Creation and Commercial Value: Copyright Protection of Works of Information,* 90 COLUM. L. REV. 1865, 1880-81 (1990). These cases generally involved commercial, competitive uses (although sometimes in related or potential, rather than directly overlapping, markets).

[236] *See infra* section VII. G.

particular, an approach that differed significantly from the model of the European directive might not trigger reciprocal protection for U.S. databases in the member states. Finally, as discussed below, the two models may have differing constitutional implications.

Nevertheless, choosing one model or the other would only be the beginning. Much would turn on the precise delineation of either approach—how the scope of the rights are defined, or what conduct is proscribed. Many of the questions raised in the discussion of the remaining issues below would still need to be resolved.

As discussed above in section IV.B, the European Commission began with an unfair competition model, but ultimately adopted a property rights model in its Directive. The Commission has given several reasons for its change in approach, primarily: (1) the lack of established unfair competition laws in every country; (2) the need for producers to know what they own ahead of time, rather than waiting until someone engages in a use which a court finds wrongful; and (3) the commercial transferability of property rights.[237]

Proponents prefer the property rights model for these and other reasons. While their greatest concern may be unfair commercial conduct, and protection against free-riding, they point out that serious damage can be caused by an irresponsible user even without the elements of competition or profit. Proponents also are reluctant to rely on the existing state law misappropriation doctrine, given its checkered and ambiguous history. Their specific dissatisfactions with the *Motorola* formulation are described in more detail above.[238]

Among the opposing groups, and some neutral groups with specific concerns, there was a strong preference for the unfair competition model. While some felt that no need had been established for any legislation, and that it was preferable to let the courts continue to develop the common law, they were less uncomfortable with the former model than the latter. A number of

---

[237] See Submission from the European Community and its Member States to the World Intellectual Property Organization on "An International Treaty on the Protection of Databases," p. 2 (July 1997).

[238] *See supra* section VII.B.5.

the concerns they expressed with regard to last year's proposals appeared to be ameliorated by such an approach. The more limited the formulation of unfair competition, and the closer to the Second Circuit's formulation in *Motorola*, the less objectionable some found it.

A few participants sought as much specificity as possible. They wished to avoid the uncertainty inherent in a general mandate to the courts to prevent conduct determined to be unfair. They urged that Congress take care not to adopt a law which would lead to litigation in every case over the legitimacy of the purpose for which data was taken. One scholar has suggested that users as well as producers would benefit from a clear statute establishing what types of use are and are not permissible, rather than continuing to rely on an ill-defined, potentially overbroad judge-made doctrine.[239]

D.   Definitions

During the meetings, there was extensive discussion of the definitions used in the draft WIPO treaty and in last year's bill. In particular, participants focused on the definitions of "database," "substantial investment," and "substantial part" or its converse, "insubstantial part." While it was not assumed that the language from either of these proposals would be used this year, similar definitional issues may arise with any new proposals.

The definition of "database" raises the question of what exactly is the subject matter to be protected—a question that is integrally related to the nature and scope of the protection. All who commented on this question agreed that it is important to define the subject matter in such a way as not to sweep too broadly, and cover material that is not intended to be covered. Many pointed out that it is difficult to articulate a precise enough definition; some believed it to be impossible. There was substantial criticism of the definition of "database" in H.R. 3531 on this ground.

---

[239] *See* Ginsburg, *supra* note 70. In this regard, it is interesting to note the reason for Justice Brandeis's dissent in *INS v. AP*. He believed that a remedy should exist for INS's conduct, but that such a claim should be provided by the legislature rather than by court-established common law. 248 U.S. at 267.

The following range of concerns was expressed: A broad definition, focusing on the collection of data in a systematic or accessible way, could be read to cover virtually everything in digital form. Even a motion picture or novel might qualify, as a systematically organized collection of 0s and 1s. Other collections of information, not ordinarily thought of as databases, might fall within the definition, such as on-line scientific discussions, scientific papers presenting research results, or an art historian's slide collection placed on-line. Computer programs, which are defined in the Copyright Act as a "set of statements or instructions," could be covered.[240]

Moreover, various building blocks of the Internet might be considered to qualify as databases, such as web sites, routing tables, domain name servers and interface specifications. If so, free access to these building blocks could be impaired, hindering interoperability and impeding the functioning of the Internet.

The video rental industry has a specific concern that the definition could cover videotapes, digital video disks, videogames or multimedia works generally, for example where a disk contains a movie combined with several previews or advertisements. Depending on how the form of protection was structured,[241] the result of including such items within the definition could be to establish for the first time in U.S. law a rental right for audiovisual works, making it impossible for companies like Blockbuster to continue their current rental business without obtaining licenses. It was suggested that one way to resolve this concern might be to require a minimum number of items to be collected in order for the collection to qualify as a database.[242]

---

[240] *See* 17 U.S.C. § 101 (definition of "computer program"). In response to such concerns, the European Directive, the WIPO Draft Treaty and H.R. 3531 each included some form of a carve-out for computer programs. Database Directive art. 1(3); WIPO Draft Treaty art. 1(4); H.R. 3531 § 3(d).

[241] If, for example, rental was not included within the scope of any protection granted, this concern would not be a problem.

[242] *Cf.* Compendium, § 307.01 (establishing minimum numerical requirement of more than three items for work to be registered as compilation).

The scientific and educational communities in particular stressed the need to ensure that government data did not fall within the definition of protected subject matter. They believe this is even more important in the context of data than in the context of copyrightable subject matter. This goal could be accomplished through a specific exclusion, similar to that provided by H.R. 3531. The bill excluded databases produced by any government, in broader terms than the exclusion for U.S. government works in the Copyright Act,[243] covering state and local governments as well as federal. Other possibilities would be an explicit exclusion of databases produced for the government by independent contractors as well as employees, or otherwise produced through the use of government funding, or databases produced by a private entity using data obtained from the government on an exclusive basis.[244] In considering this issue, it should be borne in mind that some databases are created by international partnerships, and that treatment of government data may vary from country to country.

Proponents do not seek to protect government data itself, but stress the importance of providing incentives to private entities to create new, useful databases by investing in adding value to government data.[245]

The definition of "substantial investment" raises the issue of the criterion for protection. What kind of investment, and how much, should be required? The major concern expressed in the meetings related to the situation where someone takes a preexisting collection of data, and by adding limited value to it, obtains legal rights. This was identified as particularly problematic in the context of a private party adapting government or other public domain data in some way, involving no meaningful contribution of skill, judgment, or even effort, such as formatting or

---

[243] 17 U.S.C. § 105.

[244] *See* discussion of sole source databases *infra* section VII.F.

[245] The OCLC database, for example, discussed *supra* in section III.B.1, adds value to Library of Congress catalogue records available through the Government Printing Office by providing codes identifying libraries around the world that have a given work in their collections.

adding page numbers, and then asserting control over its use. A number of participants stressed that significant added value should be required in order to obtain rights (and that the underlying information must remain available to others).

This issue is related to the question of duration, discussed below. If every new substantial investment qualifies a database for a new term of protection, the question of what constitutes a substantial investment is critical to how long protection will last. A low standard that requires only automated updating or reformatting could allow perpetual protection with little public benefit to justify it. On the other hand, a standard that is extremely high could obviate incentives for making expensive investments in researching and checking the information on a timely basis, and result in less useful databases.

The definition of "substantial part," or its converse, "insubstantial part," raises the issue of the scope of protection—i.e., what can be taken without implicating the legal rights. The European directive as well as the WIPO and legislative proposals last year provided protection against the taking of all or a substantial part of a database, excluding insubstantial portions from protection in themselves.[246] This aspect of database protection is critical in ensuring that ordinary consumer or research use will be permissible without the need to obtain consent. Under all three prior models, a student could locate and extract from a database particular items of interest to him or her without implicating the producer's rights.

In several of the Copyright Office meetings, concern was expressed that the terms used were vague, and that the taking of a single piece or small subset of data, if it were important or valuable, could be found by a court to be qualitatively substantial. The question was asked, for example, whether all sports scores from one particular game would be substantial. In addition, the WIPO draft treaty and H.R. 3531 each contained an exception to the general exclusion of insubstantial parts, in circumstances where those parts are accumulated in such a way as to affect

---

[246] Directive art. 8(1); WIPO Draft Treaty art. 2(v); H.R. 3531 §§ 2 (defining "insubstantial part") and 5(a) (1996).

the market for the database.[247] Journalists and educators in particular were concerned about the possible impact of such an exception on news gathering and educational activities.

In response to the questions raised about the meaning of "substantial" and "insubstantial," proponents point out that courts regularly interpret concepts of quantitative and qualitative "substantiality" and "materiality" in dealing with copyright and other bodies of law.

A few participants in the meetings suggested that some or all of the definitional questions could be avoided if an unfair competition model was chosen rather than a property rights model. By focusing on the nature of the conduct and the harm caused, rather than on the process of collecting the material itself, it might not be necessary to define precisely what material is and is not subject to protection.

E.   Public Interest Uses

One fundamental concern was articulated by virtually all of the groups we met with that described themselves at least in part as database users. They identified certain activities with public interest elements that they urged should be allowed to continue without new restrictions on the ability to use data or new costs in doing so—primarily scientific, research and educational activities and news reporting. Each of these activities may span the range from non-profit to commercial in nature. Particular concern was expressed about the use of government and scientific data, sports statistics and financial data.

Analytically, there are various ways in which this concern could be addressed. One possibility relates to the form of protection chosen; depending on how it is articulated, a statute based on unfair competition is likely not to cover many such activities. If an exclusive property

---

[247] *See supra* sections IV.C and V.

95

rights model is chosen instead, the scope of the rights granted could be drafted in such a way as to exclude such activities as appropriate.[248]

The exclusion from protection of insubstantial portions of a database helps but does not fully resolve the problem. While much education, research and reporting may rely on individual facts or small subsets of information, in some circumstances users need to extract substantial portions or all of a database in order to analyze its contents and draw conclusions. Thus, scientists often must analyze entire data sets in order to make findings and corroborate the research results of others, and may need to republish the background research for credibility. Public advocacy groups or reporters may need to examine substantial portions of a database to understand fully the scope of an issue.

Another possibility would be to provide an explicit exception or exceptions to cover those activities that Congress decides should be permitted without the need to obtain authorization. This could be accomplished through a broad, general exception similar to the fair use defense in copyright law; through detailed, specific exceptions more like the exceptions to a copyright owner's rights embodied in sections 108-121 of the Copyright Act; or through a combination of the two approaches.

A fair use-type approach provides several advantages. It is familiar and well-developed through judicial interpretation in the copyright context; it allows tremendous flexibility in adapting to particular factual circumstances;[249] and it fits easily within the framework of guidelines for exceptions to rights within existing international intellectual property treaties.[250] On the other

---

[248] *Cf.* H.R. 3531 § 4(a) (right is violated only by use "that conflicts with the database owner's normal exploitation of the database or adversely affects the actual or potential market for the database").

[249] The copyright fair use doctrine allows distinctions to be drawn between commercial and non-profit types of use, while recognizing that even the former may in appropriate circumstances qualify as fair. *See, e.g.*, Sega Enters. Ltd. v. Accolade, Inc., 977 F.2d 1510 (9th Cir. 1992).

[250] *See* Berne Convention, art. 9(2); TRIPs, art. 13; WIPO Copyright Treaty, art. 10; WIPO Performances and Phonograms Treaty, art. 16. While the limitations on exceptions in these treaties may not apply to *sui generis* database protection, they represent a general approach toward exceptions that has

hand, there are disadvantages too. A fair-use type approach is unpredictable in its outcome in any given case, and therefore gives little certainty to users. It could also make the new form of protection appear more like copyright, raising the potential constitutional issue discussed below in section VII.G.

The specific exemptions approach presents the flip side of many of these advantages and disadvantages.

Finally, some have suggested the possibility of compulsory licenses for certain socially favored types of uses.[251] The rationale is that this would ensure the availability of data, while enabling the setting of a reasonable price. As a general rule, compulsory licenses are not favored in intellectual property law, which ordinarily relies on the marketplace, allowing rightholders freely to negotiate terms with users.[252] In some circumstances, however, Congress has found such licenses appropriate, typically where there is a new, struggling industry that Congress decides to assist, or some practical difficulty in achieving a negotiated solution.[253]

This leads to the question whether the marketplace can appropriately handle non-profit scientific and educational uses. Some databases are produced specifically for this market; others have both commercial and non-profit uses. As described in section II above, many database producers today engage in differential pricing. That is, they provide different terms for different types of uses, generally making databases available for much lower prices to nonprofit, scientific, library or educational users than to commercial users. In essence, the commercial users subsidize the non-commercial, allowing the producer to make a profit or at least cover costs. It is unclear

---

achieved international acceptance.

[251] *See* Reichman & Samuelson, *supra* note 145, at 146-148.

[252] *See, e.g.,* Paul Goldstein, *Preempted State Doctrines, Involuntary Transfers and Compulsory Licenses: Testing the Limits of Copyright*, 24 U.C.L.A. L. REV. 1107, 1135-36 (1977) .

[253] *See, e.g.,* 17 U.S.C. §§ 111, 115 and 119. One approach taken has been to provide for compulsory arbitration if the parties cannot agree as to royalty rates and terms. *See, e.g.,* 17 U.S.C. § 115(c)(3)(D).

whether or not enacting a new form of protection would alter this practice, or tend to raise prices overall, making access to data less affordable.

F.   Duration

How long should protection last? All agree that, in theory, it should last just long enough to provide adequate incentives by allowing a fair return on investment. The difficulty lies in determining how long that period is. As with any form of intangible creation, it is complicated by the fact that different types of databases may need different terms to ensure a fair return. An extremely popular database of current and volatile data may recover costs in a much shorter time than an historical database requiring extensive research and appealing to a specialized audience. The challenge is to devise a term that works across the board, in order to encourage the production of all types of databases.

A number of possibilities have been suggested.[254] The longest is the 25-year term proposed in last year's bill.[255] The European directive requires a term of 15 years. The "catalogue rule" now in existence in some Nordic countries sets a term of 10 years. The "misappropriation" doctrine as set out in *INS* and *Motorola* suggests that protection may last as long as the data has value or as long as it is "hot"—i.e., new and timely. Such a term could vary for different databases, depending on the nature of the data, the particular market, and the state of communications technology. For example, stock prices today may be valuable or "hot" for only

---

[254] Professors Reichman and Samuelson have suggested a combination of a short initial term, followed by a period where various compulsory licenses are in effect for different types of uses. *See* Reichman & Samuelson, *supra* note 145, at 147-48.

[255] This term is considerably shorter than the term of protection for copyright. Most databases are works made for hire, and their copyright term would therefore last for seventy-five years from publication or one hundred years from creation, whichever expires first. 17 U.S.C. § 302(c).

fifteen minutes, while pre-television news from the front in World War I may have been "hot" for 24 hours or more.[256]

The discussion so far has dealt with the basic, initial term. The more difficult aspect of duration relates to changes made in a database, for example in the process of updating or verifying its contents. Proponents of legislation argue that a database should be protected as long as its producer continues to make substantial investments in maintaining it. For some databases, they report that producers spend many millions of dollars a year in updating and verifying the information they contain. They assert that there are equivalent public policy justifications for providing incentives to invest in keeping an existing database comprehensive, timely and accurate.

Last year's bill dealt with this issue by providing that "any change of commercial significance" to an existing database, including by making additions, deletions or verifications, qualified the changed database for its own new term of protection.[257] The WIPO draft treaty narrowed this language by adding the phrase "which constitute a new substantial investment" (the criterion for protection under the treaty).[258] These provisions were controversial because they could be read to create a system of perpetual protection; as long as a database continued to be updated, new terms of protection could attach *ad infinitum*. This raised both policy and constitutional questions. Should Congress create a form of intangible property that could last forever? And would doing so violate the "limited times" restriction in the Copyright Clause of the Constitution?[259]

It also raised the question of what level of investment would be sufficient to qualify for an additional term. If the threshold is too low, there may be little justification for such extended

---

[256] *See* International News Serv. v. Associated Press, 248 U.S. 215 (1918).

[257] H.R. 3531§ 6(b).

[258] Draft Database Treaty, arts. 1(1), 8(3). *Cf.* Database Directive, art. 10(3) ("Any substantial change . . . which would result in the database being considered to be a substantial new investment").

[259] U.S. CONST. art. I, § 8, cl. 8 (1789). *See* discussion *infra* section VII.G.1.

protection (particularly given the ease of making modifications in the digital age). If the requisite "substantial investment" is defined to be high enough, however, and the same level of investment is made that would qualify a new database for an initial term of protection, the argument has been made that protection should not be ruled out, simply because the comparable investment was made in updating and maintaining an existing database rather than creating a new one.

This treatment of changes made to existing databases parallels the treatment of changes to existing works of authorship in copyright law. When such a work is created today, it generally receives an initial term of protection measured by the life of the author plus fifty years.[260] If someone lawfully makes changes to the work that in themselves qualify as creative authorship, the result is a derivative work, which is entitled to its own term of protection of life plus fifty.[261] The result is not perpetual protection, however; the Copyright Act states explicitly that this new term of protection is independent of and does not affect or enlarge the duration of any copyright in the preexisting work.[262]

One way to dispel the specter of perpetual protection might be to make explicit in any database legislation that the term of protection for the preexisting database is not extended when a new term attaches to a changed version. This would clarify the problem conceptually, and ensure that protection would expire in due course for the old version of the database. Thus, for example, if the West Publishing Company published a new version of its Federal Reporter series, with corrections to some older cases and incorporating new decisions, it would receive a full term of protection for the new version. Anyone would be free, however, to copy in its entirety the prior version of the series, once its set term of years had expired (if it was not protected by copyright).

---

[260] 17 U.S.C. § 304.

[261] *Id.* §§ 101 (defining "derivative work"), 103(a).

[262] *Id.* § 103(b).

The remaining problem is a practical one. This solution will work for databases like the West reporters, to the extent that they are available in their original form. Databases available only on-line, however, may be constantly refreshed and not available to the public in their older form. Moreover, it may be impossible to determine which aspects of the database are new and which aspects were found in the prior version. The same problem exists today under copyright law. If the original work is not available, the fact that its term of protection has expired may not help a would-be user who has access only to a derivative work, particularly in situations where the preexisting material cannot easily be separated from the new matter.

It has been suggested that this issue too might be resolved by the choice of an unfair competition model rather than a property rights model. Again, the focus would be on fairness and commercial harm, rather than on the nature of the material taken. Protection could exist for as long as an investment of continued value was being taken unfairly.[263]

G.   Sole Source Data

In theory, the answer to many of the concerns that have been expressed about restricting the availability of data is that, regardless of what model of protection is chosen, the database producer would not own the data in itself. The producer's rights would extend to its own particular database as an entity, but not the items collected in the database. In other words, anyone would remain free to obtain all of the same data from other sources. Thus, the legal protection would ensure that the database maker could protect the fruits of its investment in collecting and presenting data, but would leave others able to make their own collection of the

---

[263] A comparison might be drawn to another branch of unfair competition, trademark law, under which rights exist as long as a mark continues to be used in commerce and to have value in identifying the source of the goods or services. *See* 15 U.S.C. §§ 1051, 1059 (Lanham Act §§ 1, 9).

same data. No participant at the meetings expressed disagreement with the concept of such a limitation, which could be explicitly stated in any legislation.[264]

Nevertheless, there are circumstances in which this answer alone may be unsatisfactory. When the data is not available elsewhere, the ability to prevent its extraction from the database may in effect amount to ownership of the data itself. The two prototypical examples of "sole source" data contained in a database are (1) government data provided to a private producer on an exclusive basis; and (2) data generated by the database maker itself. Included in the latter category are telephone subscriber information, sports statistics, and trading data from financial markets.[265] Unless the producer chooses to make such data freely available, it is simply not possible for anyone else to obtain it independently.[266]

This is a complex issue, involving diverse types of databases and touching on a wide variety of policy implications. We present here some general points raised in the meetings as a preliminary stage in the analysis.

A variety of mechanisms have been proposed to deal with sole source databases. Broadly categorized, they are: exclusions from protection; compulsory licenses; and regulation through

---

[264] *Cf.* H.R. 3531 § 5(b) ("[N]othing in this Act shall in any way restrict any person from independently collecting, assembling or compiling works, data or materials from sources other than a database subject to this Act"); defense of "independent creation" in copyright law. *See, e.g.,* Mazer v. Stein, 347 U.S. 201, 218 (1954) ("Absent copying there can be no infringement of copyright").

[265] Other examples mentioned in the meetings included situations where the database producer may be the only entity in possession of the underlying information, for example where the original source no longer exists or has not retained the information; and situations where information may be available elsewhere but not in the "official" form demanded by users, such as sports league statistics or legal citations. *Cf.* H.R. 1584 and H.R. 1822, 104th Cong., 1st Sess. (1995) (barring, under certain circumstances, Federal and State courts and agencies from requiring a single citation form in which copyright subsists).

[266] We do not suggest that all of the examples given should be treated in the same way. Different types of sole source data may raise different considerations, particularly with regard to the degree of justification for protection and the degree of need for access. Sports statistics in particular may be available as a practical matter through a variety of sources because the games are widely disseminated by television and radio broadcasts. *See, e.g.,* NBA v. Motorola, Inc., 105 F.3d (2d Cir. 1997) (scores obtained by defendant from television and radio).

other bodies of law such as antitrust or industry-specific government oversight. A combination of these approaches could also be considered, allowing greater fine-tuning to the nature of the database and its market.

A complete exclusion from protection is the most drastic approach, as it will result in a loss of the legal incentive to produce the database in question. This approach therefore implies a policy decision not to provide such an incentive for that type of database, and the absence of suitable, less drastic alternatives to ensure the availability of data.

The least controversial case for an exclusion from protection is the category of government data made available to the database producer on an exclusive basis. This issue implicates general U.S. policies about the conditions on which government data is made available to the public. Under current law, federal agencies are generally prohibited from entering into exclusive or restricted agreements for distribution of public information "that interferes with [its] timely and equitable availability to the public."[267] Nevertheless, the statute contains some exceptions, and other countries have different rules. The policy favoring free access to government data could be undermined if a single entity were permitted to control access through its database, with the public unable to obtain the data directly from the government or any third-party provider.[268] This result could be avoided by broadening any statutory exclusion of databases

---

[267] 44 U.S.C. § 3506(d)(4).

[268] Under current law the data usually remains available from the government, but without the added value provided by the private sector producer. Government contracts for the publication of information generally require a continued non-exclusive license for the government to use the information and make it available to others, and may also require the producer to provide the information to the government in a more accessible form (e.g., automated). For example, the catalogue entries for copyright registrations from 1978 to date are available on-line through the Library of Congress. Those records are also available in a more accessible, user-friendly form from DIALOG Information Services, Inc., which provides a powerful search engine to its users.

created by a government entity to encompass databases created from government data that has been made available on exclusive terms to the database producer.[269]

The compulsory license approach may be seen as a middle ground, allowing producers to benefit financially from the use of their products but removing their ability to control the nature or price of the use. As discussed above, however, compulsory licenses are generally disfavored in intellectual property law, and adopted only as a last resort in circumstances where the free market does not function well. The idea of a compulsory license for sole source databases was proposed in Europe in the initial stages of the database directive, but abandoned as part of an overall compromise when it proved controversial.[270]

The third possibility is to deal with this issue as a question of appropriate government control of business activities. This could be done through the application of antitrust law generally, or through regulation of a particular industry, such as through the Federal Communications Commission for the telecommunications industry or through the Securities Exchange Commission for securities markets. These are areas where Congress has determined that a regulatory scheme is advisable in order to balance the interests of the industries and the public.

An example of the antitrust approach is the *Magill* decision in the European Court of Justice, which held that television broadcasters could not rely on their compilation copyrights to prevent the copying of self-generated programming information by others wishing to publish

---

[269] The related issue of how to treat arrangements that are exclusive not as a legal matter but *de facto* is discussed below.

[270] *See* discussion *supra* section IV.B.

competing television program guides.[271] Reliance on such competition law represents the route taken, at least at present, by the European Union.[272]

As to telephone subscriber information, Congress has already acted to ensure that this information is accessible to others. The Telecommunications Act of 1996 requires telecommunications carriers to provide non-discriminatory access to telephone numbers and directory listings.[273] A number of participants in the Copyright Office meetings urged that this legislative compromise not be reversed or undermined by any new database legislation. One way to address their concern would be an explicit safeguard clause stating that nothing in the legislation affects that provision of the Telecommunications Act.[274]

Sports statistics, including the scores of individual games, is a topic that has elicited a great deal of concern, as well as litigation. Specifically, the view has been expressed that sports leagues and teams should not be able to prevent others from reporting on and communicating these facts. Those expressing this view include newspapers, broadcasters and consumers as well as those in the business of compiling and marketing such information. Stock exchange trading information presents similar issues. It may be important for news organizations or financial

---

[271] Radio Telefis Eireann v. European Commission, Court of Justice of the European Communities [1995] All ER 416, [1995] FSR 530 (April 6, 1995). Similar antitrust claims have been made by defendants in copyright infringement cases in the United States, with mixed success. The defendant in *Feist*, for example, successfully asserted an antitrust counterclaim in the district court. Rural Tel. Serv. Co. v. Feist Publications, Inc., 737 F. Supp. 610 (D. Kan. 1990). That judgment was overturned on appeal. 957 F. 2d 765 (10th Cir. 1992).

[272] *See supra,* section IV.B.

[273] Telecommunications Act of 1996, Pub. L. No. 104-104, § 222(e), 110 Stat. 56, 61, 62 (1996) (codified at 47 U.S.C. § 222(e)).

[274] *Cf.* H.R. 3531, § 9(c) ("Nothing in this Act shall prejudice provisions concerning copyright, rights related to copyright or any other rights or obligations in the database or its contents, including laws in respect of patent, trademark, design rights, antitrust or competition, trade secrets, data protection and privacy, access to public documents, and the law of contract").

analysts to be able to report and transmit information about current stock prices, available only through the services of the particular exchange.

For both of these examples, the timeliness of the data is likely to be critical, given the audiences for information as the game is played, or for prices for immediate purchase. Another variable is the extent to which others have a legitimate need to extract more than an insubstantial amount of such information—i.e., not just trading prices of particular stocks, or the outcome of the third inning of a game.

Finally, arguments have been made for special treatment of databases which are not literally sole sources, but may be the only economically feasible sources of particular data. While others can in theory independently obtain the data elsewhere, doing so is prohibitively expensive or economically wasteful. This may be the case where the data requires substantial time and effort to obtain or the database has a narrow niche market (such as a small scientific subspecialty), and no other producer has the resources or ability meaningfully to compete with a first comer. The greatest area of concern expressed is the database produced by a single producer from government data, where the data is not made available by the government in usable form. Although federal agencies are prohibited from awarding exclusive contracts for this purpose, in many cases the reality may be that only one producer enters into a contract for a particular set of data.

Such databases appear to present somewhat different policy questions than literally sole source databases. On the one hand, there is a public interest in easier, cheaper access to data for users. On the other hand, presumably in these circumstances the database producer has had to make a proportionally higher investment to obtain the data, or take greater risks. It may be that the markets for such databases cannot support more than one producer. It is unclear whether granting new legal protection will change these circumstances, either exacerbating a lack of competition or encouraging more.

On the sole source issue too, the form and scope of any new protection may be key. Within the context of an unfair competition model, the use of such a database for non-competitive purposes may be permissible. Moreover, the misappropriation doctrine could allow distinctions based on the "hotness" of the data, giving its producer some lead time in exploiting the market, but then making the data available for third-party use. If one adopts a property rights model instead, the question will be the scope of the rights and how any exceptions are drawn.

H.   **Constitutionality**

One other set of issues requires consideration, although they were not discussed in depth at the Copyright Office meetings: the constitutional implications of any new legislation in this area. Two primary issues have been identified: (1) possible constraints imposed on Congressional power to legislate in this area by the language of the Copyright Clause;[275] and (2) First Amendment limitations. We provide here an outline of the nature of the problems rather than an in-depth analysis.

1.   *Copyright Clause*

The Copyright Clause imposes certain restrictions on Congress's ability to enact copyright legislation. The text itself makes clear that copyrights cannot be of indefinite duration, but can only be granted "for limited times." In addition, the Supreme Court in *Feist* held that Congress could not constitutionally provide copyright protection based on "sweat of the brow," but could only protect works of authorship embodying a modicum of creativity. The questions are then whether Congress can provide protection for "sweat" or investment without creativity under a different Article I power, most likely under the Commerce Clause,[276] and whether any such

---

[275] U.S. CONST., art. I, sec. 8, cl. 8 (authorizing Congress to grant copyrights and patents by giving it the power "to promote the Progress of Science and Useful Arts, by securing for limited Times to Authors and Inventors the exclusive Right to their respective Writings and Discoveries.") [hereinafter, the *Copyright Clause*].

[276] U.S. CONST., art. I, sec. 8, cl. 3.

protection must incorporate a limited term. The answers to these questions are not entirely clear. They may depend in part on the form of protection that is chosen, and the extent to which it differs from copyright in both end and means.

It has long been accepted that Congress has the power to enact trademark legislation under the Commerce Clause, despite the fact that trademarks may be seen as a form of intellectual property; that trademark law protects material that does not meet standards for copyright or patent protection; and that the protection may last indefinitely. The Supreme Court's opinion in *The Trademark Cases*[277] held unconstitutional an early attempt by Congress to enact a trademark law, based on a lack of Congressional power under either the Copyright Clause or the Commerce Clause. According to the Court, the Copyright Clause did not provide authority for the legislation because trademarks have different "essential characteristics" from inventions or writings, since they are the result of use (often of already-existing material) rather than invention or creation, and do not depend on novelty or originality.[278] The Commerce Clause did not provide authority because the law governed *all* commerce and was not limited to interstate or foreign commerce, "the kind of commerce which Congress is authorized to regulate."[279] The opinion suggests that similar legislation limited as to the type of commerce involved would pass constitutional muster under the Commerce Clause. Indeed, such legislation was subsequently enacted and has continued unchallenged since 1905.

To the extent that database protection promotes different policies from copyright protection, and does so in a different manner, it is similar to trademark law, and therefore seems likely to survive a constitutional challenge.

---

[277] 100 U.S. 82 (1879).

[278] *Id.* at 93-94.

[279] *Id.* at 97.

Some doubt is created, however, by a 1982 Supreme Court decision dealing with the interaction of the Commerce Clause with another enumerated Article I power of Congress, the Bankruptcy Clause. In *Railway Labor Executives' Association v. Gibbons*,[280] the Court struck down a statute enacted to provide protection to the employees of a railroad in bankruptcy, on the ground that this was prohibited by the "uniformity" requirement of the Bankruptcy Clause, and Congress could not evade this prohibition by legislating under the Commerce Clause. The opinion therefore suggests that Congress cannot necessarily rely on the generality of the Commerce Clause to evade specific restrictions set out in other enumerated powers.[281]

Nevertheless, it seems possible to distinguish *Railway Labor*, and reconcile it with the implications of *The Trademark Cases*. In *Railway Labor*, the statute at issue by its terms regulated the administration of a bankruptcy, so that the Commerce Clause was being used to enact a bankruptcy statute without abiding by the restrictions of the Bankruptcy Clause. Protecting the investment in databases may be seen as distinct from protecting original authorship through copyright, and therefore avoid running afoul of the specific restrictions in the Copyright Clause. In *Feist* itself, the Court suggested that protection for "sweat" could appropriately be provided under a different legal theory, despite the fact that it could not be provided under copyright law. If, however, database legislation appears to be the equivalent of copyright under another name, but providing protection to uncopyrightable subject matter for unlimited times, the use of a different label and the recitation of a different constitutional basis will not alone be sufficient to save it. In sum, the more the statute differs from copyright, the more likely it is to be constitutional.

This is not to say that only an unfair competition model would pass constitutional muster. While an unfair competition statute seems most clearly to avoid Copyright Clause problems, it is

---

[280] 455 U.S. 457 (1982).

[281] *See* Jane C. Ginsburg, *No 'Sweat' ? Copyright and Other Protection of Works of Information After Feist v. Rural Telephone*, 92 COLUM. L. REV. 338, 370 (1992).

possible that a new but sufficiently distinct form of property right could also fall within Congressional Commerce Clause power.

2.   *First Amendment*

The First Amendment must also be kept in mind in considering any new database protection legislation. To the extent that the legislation restricts the communication of facts, it might implicate First Amendment values.

Because copyright restricts the use of expression, it also has the potential to raise First Amendment problems. The courts have held, however, that copyright law accommodates First Amendment values through the idea/expression dichotomy and the fair use doctrine.[282]

Depending on the model chosen and the formulation adopted for any database legislation, it might be advisable to include an explicit statutory provision clarifying that individual facts are not protected.[283] If individual facts remain free to be used for purposes of expression, whether political, artistic or other, there may be little need from a First Amendment perspective to copy a substantial portion of an entire database. To the extent that making a statement requires the use of more than a few facts, the form of protection and the nature and scope of the statutory exceptions would be highly relevant.

---

[282] *See* Harper & Row, Publishers, Inc. v. Nation Enters., 471 U.S. 539, 560 (1985).

[283] *Cf.* 17 U.S.C. § 102(b).